T0288957

WHEN THE WILD CALLS

WHEN THE WILD CALLS

Wilderness Reflections from a Sportsman's Notebook

JACK KULPA

TAYLOR TRADE PUBLISHING

Lanham • New York • Dallas • Boulder • Toronto • Oxford

First Taylor Trade Publishing edition 2004

This Taylor Trade Publishing hardcover edition of *When the Wild Calls* is an original publication. It is published by arrangement with the author.

Published by Taylor Trade Publishing
An imprint of The Rowman & Littlefield Publishing Group, Inc.
4501 Forbes Boulevard, Suite 200
Lanham, Maryland 20706

Distributed by National Book Network

Library of Congress Cataloging-in-Publication Data

Kulpa, Jack.
When the wild calls : wilderness reflections from a sportsman's notebook / Jack Kulpa.
p. cm.
ISBN 1-58979-123-1 (hardcover : alk. paper)
1. Natural history—Anecdotes. 2. Fishing—Anecdotes. 3. Hunting—Anecdotes. 4. Kulpa, Jack. I. Title.
QH81.K87 2004
508—dc22
2003015072

The paper used in this publication meets the minimum requirements of American National Standard for Information Sciences—Permanence of Paper for Printed Library Materials, ANSI/NISO Z39.48–1992.
Manufactured in the United States of America.

This book is for Peggy

Contents

Acknowledgments xi

Foreword: When the Wild Calls xiii

Part One: Lakes and Streams

1 Time on the Water 3

2 The Mist People 7

3 Lakes of the Rainbow Woods 13

4 Promises to Keep 19

5 The Lonely Land 23

6 The November Season 29

7 The End of the Trail 35

8 The Everlasting 41

Part Two: Forests and Fields

9 The Solitude Hunter 47

10 Keeper of the Flame 55

11 Bogtrotter 61

12 Stolen Hours 65

13 Wild Goose Chase 69

14 Just One More 75

15 Root River 81

16 Burning Bright 85

Part Three: Tail Feathers and Backlash

17 Fishing with Bubba 91

18 The Bear Facts 99

19 The Compleat Idler 105

20 Nailin' Toads 109

21 A Sportsman's Lifetime Reading List 117

22 Deercampsia Hypomnesia 121

23 Sports Show 129

24 Mr. Majestik 133

Part Four: Home from the Hill

25 A Place in the Woods 141

26 Mementos 149

27 The Trail Not Taken 155

28 The Spook in the Timber 159

29 By Dawn's Early Light 163

30 Bridges 167

31 Home from the Hill 171

32 The Secret of Chequah-Bikwaki 177

About the Author 183

Acknowledgments

Much of the material in this book appeared—sometimes slightly altered, and occasionally under different titles—in the following magazines:

Sports Afield: "When the Wild Calls," "The Mist People," "Lakes of the Rainbow Woods," "The End of the Trail," "The Solitude Hunter," "Wild Goose Chase," "The Secret of Chequah-Bikwaki," "Fishing with Bubba," and "Mr. Majestik."

Field & Stream: "Time on the Water," "The Everlasting," "Keeper of the Flame," "Just One More," "Burning Bright," "Nailin' Toads," and "Deercampsia Hypomnesia."

Wisconsin Outdoor Journal: "The Compleat Idler," "Sports Show," and "The Trail Not Taken."

Wisconsin Sportsman: "The Bear Facts."

Sporting Classics: "A Place in the Woods."

"The Lonely Land" was originally published in *Wisconsin Trails* magazine.

The people to whom I owe much are many and far-flung, but there are some to whom I am especially indebted: Kim Leslie of Taylor Trade, for suggesting this book; Chuck Wechsler of *Sporting Classics* for his enthusiasm and support; and Peg and

Nick, my wife and son, without whom I would have accomplished nothing. Thank you.

Last—but certainly not least—I am especially grateful to my parents, Edward and Dolores Kulpa, who waited for what must have been an insufferably long time for their oldest child to grow up.

Foreword: When the Wild Calls

We were at one of those cocktail parties my wife's boss occasionally throws for his clients when suddenly I found myself knee-deep in Wisconsin's Brule River, casting for brown trout below Boxcar Hole.

It had rained the night before and the water was as cloudy as coffee and cream, but I had taken a nice fish earlier on a Mepps spinner and now I had tied into one of the Brule's big browns. The fish jumped clear of the water and when it did I could clearly see its broad sides, its brassy flanks speckled with fiery crimson. It ran away from me and toward the far bank's alder tangles; then came the tense moment as the fish tried to bore into the sweepers. But I turned it away toward open water and soon my line was slicing small circles in the current beside me. In another moment, I would slip my net under the trout.

"Honey, stop fishing," said my wife.

Suddenly I was back at the hotel in Superior, Wisconsin, in a dark-paneled room filled with attorneys and insurance adjusters. Instead of a 5-pound brown, I was holding a Beefeater martini.

"Be nice," Peg said.

"I am being nice," I protested.

"No, you're not. You're fishing. Pretend you're having fun and mingle."

I wandered over to the buffet table and the platter of smoked goose pâté, and thought about the Canadas feeding in the wild rice of Mulligan Lake not far from the headwaters of the St. Croix. It was only September but autumn was already in the air; behind our blind a clump of staghorn sumac blazed like a red lantern. The wind was backing around to the northeast and the pewter sky was filled with the gabbling of geese. We crouched in the blind, still as stone, watching as a lone bird dropped down from beneath the clouds. I could hear the air *whoosh* as the goose cupped its wings. It was going to land in our decoys.

I jumped to my feet and threw the shotgun to my shoulder, ready to back up my partner if he missed the shot.

"TAKE HIM!" I cried. "Shoot!" Then I realized the man at my elbow was wearing a gray flannel suit. He stared at me as if I were dangerous. My wife rushed up to us and touched his arm.

"Please ignore my husband," Peg told her boss. "He has these fits every now and then. They start in April when the steelhead run, and peak in November when the bluebills arrive."

I'm willing to bet you're no stranger to this sort of thing. After all, great outdoorsmen think alike—or at least share the same fantasies. You and I will be standing in line at the bank or post office while our imaginations slip away to some place we'd much rather be—a cornfield where cock pheasants are bragging loudly; a salmon stream where chinooks are leaping cascades; a lonely campsite beside a wilderness lake brimming with walleyes; a patch of aspen where the grouse grow as thick as deer flies.

Psychologists claim these mental lapses are an escape mechanism—our psyche's way of keeping us sane in a sometimes disappointing and often ludicrous world. Other people call it daydreaming, and others yet—most notably long-suffering wives—swear it's the first hint of dementia.

I think my own explanation is probably closer to the truth. To paraphrase Robert Service, you and I have probed the silent places where we've heard the wild calling—perhaps a backcountry creek from which we took brookies, a marsh where the teal streaked by like bullets, or a day when we watched November fill with the first inch of tracking snow. We know the excitement that is there wherever the wild calls, and the magical way it lingers like an echo in our memories; and when it calls—regardless of where we are or what we're doing—we slip away, in one way or another, to answer.

To be sure, the call of the wild is a haunting and elusive magic, subtle as a sunrise, fleeting as a falling star. It is in the sound of geese, in the roar of river rapids, and in the silent solitude of places that no one has visited. Like gathering wood to build a campfire, the calling is a simple and uncomplicated thing, but like the mists of a brooding bog it can also be a riddle—cryptic, deep, and filled with mystery.

Although I've been lucky enough to have known the magic in many places, I find it most easily in the big woods of the Lake Superior country. The home I've made here serves as my listening post and as a sort of base camp from which I follow the call, on foot or by canoe, into the surrounding woods. For it is here, among the wilderness lakes and boreal forests of the North, where an old and vanishing world still exists, where time is measured in seasons and sunsets, and where life remains closely linked to the past.

I have heard the call on clear winter nights, when even the stars seemed to shudder at the mournful howl of wolves, and I have seen its primitive brilliance among the northern lights, in a sky alive with the spectral dance of phantoms. But most often I've found it in the ordinary things: the pat of rain against a tent, the familiar feel of an old and favorite paddle, or in a pine knot I'd forgotten about and then found again tucked away in a pack.

And sometimes I have felt its spell long after I was gone from the wild places, when something about the weather or something that I saw stirred a memory: Then suddenly the magic was back.

I may not know many of the things an outdoorsman should know, but of this much I am certain: Wherever there are trees and rocks, fields and water, silence, solitude, joy, and wonder, there, too, I'll hear the wild calling. It's as much a man's response to the natural world as it is the quality of a place. It's what I feel in casting a line or taking a shot, and suddenly remembering what spirit really means.

* * *

I can clearly recall the first time I found the magic. I was ten years old and in those days my parents' home stood at what was then the edge of town. Beyond our door, farms and woodlots rolled away across southern Wisconsin to where a small stream lay sheltered beneath enormous oaks and elms.

That stream was a magnet for small boys like me, who went there at every opportunity to fish. Our homemade gear was crude and rugged: a green willow wand, a few feet of cotton line, a matchbox filled with perch hooks and a can of worms. Usually we caught bullheads and sometimes bluegills, and though the fish were small, each one was a thing of wonder.

It was that sense of wonder that lured me to the stream. I wondered where it came from and where it led, and what lay waiting to be discovered around the next bend. Most of all, I wondered what lay upstream past the point where we were forbidden to wander. The mystery of that unvisited land tugged at me relentlessly, and though I tried to resist it, the lure of the unknown gave me no rest.

Finally, one day when everyone else was in school, I slipped away to explore the hidden. I cached my books in a hollow stump, pocketed my lunch, and set out in search of adventure. The land was gleaming with the copper light of Indian summer. Clear skies echoed with the high calling of geese. Pheasants cackled in sere cornfields. A billowing wind moved restlessly through the trees.

I walked upstream past abandoned farms and feral apple orchards. I jumped wood ducks feeding on acorns along the banks. Eventually the stream widened into a deep, clear pool where the silence was teeming. Not a ripple marred the pool's serene surface; not a leaf quivered along its banks. I crawled up a willow that leaned out like a bridge over the water, lay down on my belly, and peered into the crystalline depths.

Bubbling springs were kicking up little spumes of gravel from the bottom; every pebble was visible and distinct. A bass lay finning against the gravel, a glistening shadow of gold and green. A gust of wind ruffled the surface of the water; colored leaves coasted like toy parachutes on the breeze. This was not the familiar stream I knew—this was something secret, magical, and pristine.

Home was only a mile or two away, but I was as alone as a boy could be. The bubbling springs, vast silence, and sense of isolation made their indelible mark on me. I was too young to understand about solitude; I only knew I'd discovered something wonderful and new. But now, a lifetime later, I know it was there, beside the pool, where the wild first called to me.

* * *

Years later, when I was a young man, I found the magic again on the maze of steelhead streams that lie west of Lake Superior's Montreal River. It was wild country, a roadless area of balsam and spruce where whitewater rivers raced with deafening speed. April was budding, but in the tamarack swamps the snow still lay waist-deep. The high, muddy streams were icy with slush, but in the air was the feel of spring.

I tossed spawn sacs and yarn flies into all the right places, along streams like the Graveyard, the Oronto, and Parker Creek. Late one afternoon I took a nice, lake-run rainbow near the mouth of the Brunsweiller, and by the time I made the trapper's shack on the Marengo River, a full moon filled the sky.

The primitive cabin was just big enough for a lone man and whatever gear he could carry. Built of rough logs, with a birch bark roof, it was as rugged and austere as a dry spot under a tree. I cooked my fish outdoors over an open fire, using a smooth log for a table and dispensing with candlelight in favor of the moon. Owls hooted madly in the surrounding dark timber, beneath a sky that blazed with the ancient light of stars. Mine was a pauper's meal as such things go, but when it was finished, more than my hunger had been filled.

My bed of balsam boughs filled the cabin's single room with its fragrance. Deer mice wandered down from the purlins to snatch bits of bread. The dirt floor was thick and spongy with rusty pine needles, and through the window I watched the Marengo mirror the moon. Surely, I thought, there was no finer place on earth; and because I was there, I was the luckiest of men.

For the first time, I saw the wisdom in Thoreau's remark to "drive life into a corner and reduce it to its simplest terms." The simplicity of the cabin was a refuge from confusion. As I lay in my blankets at night listening to the wind rattle the tin chimney, the problems of a troubled world seemed more remote than the stars. Instead, my thoughts were occupied by the calling of owls, the good stretches of trout water where others seldom ventured, and the fresh bear track I had seen in the snow beside some nameless stream. Outside the cabin, snow hissed and swirled as spruce boughs brushed against the window. There, too, the wild called to me.

* * *

Another time, while hunting grouse along the red cliffs of Lake Superior, I found the magic among the ruins of an old Indian burial ground. The graveyard was an emerald glade guarded by giant white pines, massive trees well over 300 years old. Tiny wooden houses with shingled roofs covered each gravesite, with holes cut out beneath the eaves so that the dead could travel freely between this world and the next. The houses had been built long ago to protect the graves from wolves. The wooden structures were in the last stages of decay, and it was clear no one had tended to the graves in years.

I thought of the old warriors at rest in the earth and wondered what tales lay buried with the bones. The same life that flowed through me had once flowed through them, yet the only signs of their ever having passed this way were a few crumbling wooden structures. Inexplicably, I felt linked to the men who lay forgotten in that ground, men whose lives seemed as ephemeral as the flash of a firefly in the night. I had set out that day with no other aim but to take a walk and maybe bag a grouse, yet somewhere along the way I had crossed a bridge between worlds.

The wind picked up and jostled the murmuring pines. The ancient trees made me painfully aware of my own transient life. Little shadows raced through the woods toward the quickening sunset, and one of them was mine. Here, too, I heard the wild calling, soft and sublime.

Since those early experiences, I have found the magic many times and in many places, sometimes in the company of others, but far more often when I was alone. Usually it happens when I least expect it, when, in a quiet moment out of doors, brown trout begin to rise on a moon-dappled stream, or the dusk suddenly comes to life with loon song and the swift whisper of wings. It is then I am made aware that these tangible things are only symbols of what I seek; what I really want is to be there when the wild calls and to be a part of the magic its music brings.

PART ONE

LAKES AND STREAMS

ONE

Time on the Water

Late that night, after the cribbage board was put aside and the fishing gear was made ready for the next day, we tossed a pine knot into the woodstove to keep September's chill at bay, and then settled back with the good bourbon. Our group had been friends since boyhood, back when we fished with J. C. Higgins reels. It seemed incredible that in a few years we'd be old enough to retire. Time is a thief, especially late at night in a fishing camp, when the talk turns to second-guessing the choices you've made.

"Why fish?" one of us asked, a bit querulously. "Don't you ever regret wasting so much time on the water?"

To be sure, we squandered much enthusiasm on fishing; as a result, none of us was as well heeled as he might have been. Although there was always enough money to buy the latest in graphite and Gore-Tex, our wives shopped at discount stores and clad out little ones in hand-me-downs; our oldest kids relied on part-time jobs and student loans to stay in college. None of us had ever taken the family to Disney World, though there'd been plenty of trips to Yellowstone and Canada. True, our wives claimed not to mind, and our kids were growing into highly proficient anglers who enjoyed fishing as much as we did; but by anyone's standards our accomplishments were small change—unless you counted the 6-pound brookies we'd taken on the Nipigon.

* * *

"Why fish?" The question—and perhaps the bourbon—put us in a reflective mood.

I fish because I love the silences and solitudes of wild places as much as I do the trout that lurk there. I fish for the wonder and joy I knew as a boy, and for the adventure I still believe life can be.

I fish because I don't want to fritter away my time in not-so-quiet desperation and end up an embittered old man who shouts at the TV. I fish for the enormous satisfaction of catching my supper, for the pleasurable pretense of being a woodsman living off the land, and because in releasing a 10-pound walleye I feel as magnanimous as a king. I fish not because I'm particularly good at it but because I'm equally inept at everything else. I fish because I can.

I fish because it is a gift my father gave me and that I have passed on to my son, and because without it the three of us might never have been friends. I fish because goodness and unsullied artlessness are increasingly rare, and I don't want to lose what little I've kept. I fish for the thrilling thunder of river rapids, the mournful wailing of loons, and the lure of an untrammeled forest trail that leads to a tarn . . . somewhere.

I fish because even though the wilderness is shrinking, the best water is overcrowded, and the fishing isn't what it used to be, there's always the chance that it might be different for me. I fish because there are lakes and streams that brim with reflections, where I visit with old friends who have vanished like yesterday. I fish not to escape, or meditate, or wade through midlife crises, but because in battling an enormous pike I am keenly aware of being alive.

* * *

Why fish?

Because it's the best way I know to convince youngsters that there's more to life than shopping malls. Because it's not mandatory, critical, or important—except to me. Because without it I would be a different person, and I don't think that person would be as happy.

In the end, my friends and I agreed that of all the dreams in this fickle world, only the joy of fishing remains true. A line from Wordsworth seems to convey what we tried to say: "Nature never did betray / The heart that loved her."

TWO

The Mist People

Almost everyone who has traveled the old canoe routes of the North has heard it at one time or another: the sounds and voices of people who weren't there.

It happens most often at night, after the campfire burns to embers and the tent flaps are sealed against the dark. Then, just as the images of dreams begin darting out at you from sleep, a corner of your consciousness catches the low murmur of voices, barely audible above the roar of a rapids or the sound of the wind in the trees. You listen, lying awake and alert, trying to make out the words. But the whispers remain vague and indistinct, as shadowy as the man in the moon.

The old French fur traders who first explored the Lake Superior region credited these incidents to "the mist people"—supernatural beings who haunted wild places. Known also as "the huntsmen" or "the voices of the rapids," the phenomenon usually occurred near places of quickwater, and it was here where entire camps were often routed from sleep by the sounds of phantoms passing through the night.

In their search for fur and the fabled Northwest Passage, the voyageurs dared to go where no white man had ever trod. In the 200 years following Étienne Brûlé's discovery of Lake Superior in 1623, these intrepid explorers traveled by canoe, braving hostile Indians, unmapped rivers, and attacks by rival traders. They chose life in the wilderness over a relatively comfortable existence in the villages along the St. Lawrence River from which many of them came. When asked why, their answer was always the same: "It is the riddles that make life an adventure."

But that was long ago. Today, the voyageurs are gone and much of their beloved wilderness is only a memory, banished to oblivion by a world that has no use for mystery and mirage. Yet, along the old canoe routes of those early explorers, modern-day travelers still hear the mist people murmuring in the dark.

One such place is the Bois Brule River, a whiskey-colored strand of wild and brooding water that lies at the southwest corner of Lake Superior. Known nowadays as a blue-ribbon trout stream, the Brule was once a major route of the fur trade.

One night in early May, I camped along the river after having spent the day fishing its frigid water. Too tired to pitch the tent, I rolled up in my blankets beside the campfire, shut my eyes, and listened to the sounds of the forest—the call of an owl, the sputter of the fire, the purl of the river below. I could feel consciousness slipping away like beads of water rolling down a taut line, when—*thump*—something in the darkness startled me.

I sat up, straining to hear what it was. And then, faint but clearly audible above the sounds of a rushing river, came the musical murmur of voices.

It was little more than a muffled maundering but distinct enough so that there could be no mistaking what it was: a group of men on the river below my camp talking and laughing.

Bump. As I listened to the sound of them dragging their canoes ashore, I was certain it was the group of canoeists I had met earlier that day. I rolled out of my blankets and put the coffee on the fire, expecting guests at any moment. But when I went down to the river to greet them, there was only moonlight on the water and the river chinking against the rocks like glass chimes in the wind.

I'm sure it was my imagination. And yet, ever since Radisson and Groseilliers—the architects of the Hudson Bay Company—first explored the country beyond Chequamegon Bay in 1659, white travelers to the region have reported hearing the voices. One thing is sure about the existence of the mist people, whether they be the actual whispers of phantoms or the sound of wind and water playing tricks: Nothing in the North is more fantastically unreal to tell about, and yet, when heard, nothing is more astonishingly concrete.

* * *

Curiously enough, veterans of the voyageurs' brigades were seldom alarmed by the mist people. In fact, the mist people rendered impressions of the life the voyageurs had left behind: the stony walls of a French town, its bustling marketplace, narrow streets filled with the gay laughter of peasants, the toll of church bells on a sunny Sunday morning. Seldom did the mist people speak of heartache and struggle. As one writer notes, it was as if "the nations of the earth whisper to their exiled sons through the voices of the rapids. . . . Perhaps this is the great Mother's compensation in a harsh mode of life."

And yet, eerie adventures can occur whenever the mist people speak. A friend of mine likes to tell of when he heard the ghosts along the Yellow Dog River near Lake Independence and how, at that instant, a silver-tipped black bear soundlessly walked through his camp, its coat glittering like a constellation of stars in the moonlight. Another time, not far from the old voyageurs' place of rendezvous at Grand Portage, an owl roosted from the ridgepole of our tent. I watched as the horny talons pierced the taut fabric. Even now I can remember how that menacing claw felt cold to the touch, and how, each time I raised a finger to stroke it, the big bird would suddenly bolt away into the dark, always returning to roost the moment I began drifting off to sleep again.

Strangest of all was a night I spent on the remote East Fork of the Chippewa River. We made our camp at the rapids below Pelican Lake, and all through the night some large, snarling beast kept circling the tent whenever the campfire dimmed, its guttural sounds unlike anything I had ever heard before, or since. In the morning, in a popple copse behind the tent, I found the near-fossilized jawbone of some monstrous animal. It looked as though it had come from a grotesque wolf, the elongated fangs curling back on themselves like tusks. But the bone was huge—twice the size of any wolf's skull I had ever seen—and I was sure that what I was looking at was the remains of some predatory animal that had stalked the mists when mammoths and mastodons still roamed the earth.

Years later I met an Indian at Sand Bay who had had similar experiences. I told him about what I had heard that night and how I had found the strange bone the next morning. The Indian nodded as I talked, but in the end he, too, was at a loss to explain things.

"I've heard the ghosts many times," he said, "but I can't tell you what they are. My grandfather probably would have said you were given an omen, but I don't think anybody nowadays knows what such a thing means."

I keep that bone on a shelf where I can always look at it, and each time I do I find myself back on the Chippewa River as phantom creatures snarl and hiss at me from the dark. I keep promising myself that someday I'll take the bone to a museum and have it identified, but I know I never will. I'm afraid some paleontologist will look at it and see only a bone, and hear nothing of the strange beasts and beings who called to me from the mists that night.

* * *

For some reason, many people never hear the phantoms; this was true even in the voyageurs' time. From all accounts, an experience with the mist people depended on why a man was drawn to the woods and what he hoped to find there.

I learned this during the winter I lived alone in a cabin along a northern river. The cabin had no telephone, no TV, no radio, no link at all to the world of other men, but it was exactly the kind of place I had been seeking.

I wanted the chance to live alone in the woods, to experience the kind of solitude few people ever know today. Most of all, I wanted to find out if I had missed something about life for never having lived it in solitude, and if time spent alone in a wild place could reveal any secrets about myself that I never knew or suspected. But after the first few days, the novelty of living like a recluse began to wear thin, and as the weeks passed I began to actually ache for the sound of another human voice.

"You'll go crazy livin' alone," an old trapper had warned me. "We'll find you at springtime, nutty as pecan pie." I had laughed at the remark in the beginning, but after several solitary weeks at the cabin I no longer remembered what I had found so funny.

Luckily, breakup occurred early that year, and by the first of April the woods were roaring with swollen rivers. And then one night, while lying half-awake in my bunk with the windows opened, I heard the mist people speak.

At first I was apprehensive. I had heard tales of mad trappers and other backwoods hermits who, in solitude, had heard and then surrendered to the dark side of the voices. I expected to hear the malevolent whispers of demons: yet, when curiosity finally won out, there were only the sunny sounds of human life in motion.

Soon I began looking forward to the time I could spend lying awake in my bunk listening to the murmurs from the river below. I would hear the sound of children playing outdoors on a warm summer evening; at other times it was the bright, nervous laughter of young women discussing men; some nights it was the good-natured banter of close friends on an outing; but always when I went to investigate, I found only the river and the mist.

Another man might have convinced himself that he was going crazy, but I heard only echoes of a life I had left behind. Haunted by the loneliness of my own self-imposed exile, I heard the voices of the rapids as the voyageurs had: "A gift from the great Mother, her compensation in a harsh mode of life."

* * *

There are rivers where the mist people still gather, and each time I find them I learn something more about wild places and why I am drawn to them. Like the old adventurers who first explored the North in birch bark canoes, I too am a voyageur, searching for a Northwest Passage of my own. And it's when I'm in the wild places, on those soundless, misty nights, after the tent flaps are sealed and the campfire is only embers, that I often believe I've found the way.

But then, in those moments, the mist people always speak.

I know it's an omen, but I can't divine the meaning. As the Indian said, no one nowadays knows what such things mean. Still, I lie awake in my blankets and listen. Like the jawbone I keep on a shelf, it's the riddles—and never the answers—that make life an adventure.

THREE

Lakes of the Rainbow Woods

The Rainbow Lake Wilderness Area lies almost within sight of my back door—its many lakes are as familiar to me as any I have known. One of the first federally designated wilderness areas east of the Mississippi, its virgin hemlocks shelter two dozen glistening lakes and ponds.

The Rainbow is a glimpse of what the North was like when it was young. So near in time is that world to our own that its shadow has not receded from the Rainbow's woods. Here, with miles of silence pressing in from every direction, I can cast a line anywhere and find yesterday.

No Name Lake is one of these places. It belongs to Martin, the last of the North's old-time fishing guides; his tall tales about the canoe country were as much a part of it as its lakes and streams. Martin was already an accomplished guide when, while still a boy, he canoed Calvin Coolidge and Herbert Hoover down the nearby Bois Brule River. Years later, when Martin was seventy and I was twenty, he showed me No Name Lake.

It was dusk and bass were rising along the shore. Owls called from the dark hemlocks; nearby, a pack of brush wolves yapped at the moon. We shoved off in Martin's canvas canoe, paddling across the twilight's reflections. After a while, Martin stopped and pulled out a pocket tin of Velvet tobacco to roll himself a cigarette. Then he cast his line at a log and immediately a smallmouth struck the popper. The bass was a battler, leaping into the air and dashing under our canoe until it was near enough for Martin to slip his thumb into its maw. The fish was easily 7 pounds—the biggest smallmouth bass I'd ever seen.

My jaw dropped when Martin released it.

"You look as shocked as Coolidge did whenever he'd see me release a big fish," Martin said. "He was so stunned he couldn't talk—that's why people started calling him 'Silent Cal.'"

I looked at Martin, thinking he was having his way with the truth.

"What?" he asked. "Would I lie?"

"Exaggerate, maybe," I said.

"I was born as honest as they come," Martin said. "Then I started fishing with politicians and I got over it."

Martin is gone now and canvas canoes have disappeared along with pocket tins of tobacco. Yet, whenever I come to No Name Lake, Martin is always near. It is always dusk when I return and the old guide is spinning his tales while the two of us paddle through the twilight, toward a log where Martin casts a popper, and catches the biggest smallmouth I've ever seen in the North.

* * *

Immediately adjacent to the Rainbow lies the Flynn Lake Wilderness, with many more lakes and spring-fed ponds. Like the Rainbow, mechanized travel is banned here. The woods near Wabigon Lake are especially speckled with wild and isolated pools of water. One of these ponds belongs to Reino.

We hiked deep into the woods that weekend, tossing spinners into places like Balsam Pond and Beaver Lake, before discovering Reino's "Indigo" pond. Here, in water as cold as ice, we caught blue-hued brookies that Reino dubbed "indigo trout."

Reino's grandfather was one of the Finnish pioneers who had settled the Lake Superior country in the 1920s, and every man in his clan was a logger. Reino thought of mature trees as a crop to be cut; I think he fished Indigo Pond as much for its virgin timber as he did for its trout.

Here, on a few acres of unspoiled and pristine earth, stood a remnant patch of young America—giant white pines and hemlocks that rose like columns, so tall their tops shut out the sun. Here, if anywhere, I knew what Longfellow meant when wrote, "This is the forest primeval."

"A perfectly good waste of timber," Reino said, each time we fished Indigo Pond. "Setting trees aside to rot is ridiculous. I could build an entire house from just one of these pines."

I agreed with Reino at the time and for long thereafter—until forests that were open to mechanized travel began to teem with trucks, trail bikes, and the ubiquitous ATV. "Multiple use" forest management has come to mean "no use" for those who seek a place away from machines.

Not long ago, Reino and I walked to Indigo Pond for the first time in years. The hike was much longer than we recalled, but nothing else had changed. Its lofty pines and hemlocks still rose to the sky, sheltering an icy pond as clear and flawless as a gem. The indigo trout were as blue and wild as ever, and the arduous hike made the sense of isolation complete. The only sound was the hush of a primitive place.

"Listen," Reino said.

"I don't hear anything," I told him.

Reino smiled. "Exactly! This is what my grandfather heard when he settled this land."

"I thought setting aside these trees was a waste of timber," I reminded him.

Reino grinned. "What can I tell you?" he asked. "People change."

* * *

Not far away lies Anodanta Lake. This spot belongs to Joey. He was a thirteen-year-old boy who seldom smiled, a quiet kid who was unsure of everything but the prospect of loss. He had come for a visit that summer to escape his parents' divorce.

"Do you like to fish?" I asked.

He shrugged. "I'm not very good at it."

Back home, Joey fished with other kids for carp in big city parks, but even by a child's standards his fishing stories were small potatoes.

"Take him someplace where he can catch fish," said my wife. "Who knows when he'll have the chance again?"

I'd already decided on Anodanta. Its floating mats of coontail and milfoil always produced northern pike—average fish that ran between 16 and 24 inches in length. It was where I'd taken my own son to catch pike when he was barely big enough to hold a rod. I was sure the pesky northerns would provide plenty of action for Joey.

At Anodanta we spent a few minutes on shore until Joey got the hang of tossing a weedless spoon; he acted as bored as a kid pitching paper at a waste can.

"What's wrong?" I asked.

"I never catch fish," he said. "Even when I hook a fish, I let somebody else reel it in. If I didn't, I'd lose it."

We shoved off in the canoe with Joey in the bow. Almost instantly he had a strike, and from the start I could see it was something larger than a hatchet-handle northern.

A pike as long as a log burst like a depth charge from under the coontail. It thrashed across the surface vegetation, like an animal trapped in a net. Joey's reel squealed as the fish burrowed into the milfoil, tangling the line in the weeds.

"Keep your tip up!" I started barking orders, sure that Joey would lose the fish in the weeds. In my mind, the fish was already gone. Then I realized the canoe was moving—the fish was *towing* us.

"He's huge!" I said.

Joey glanced over his shoulder at me. He looked terror-stricken. "Help me!" he cried.

"I can't reach you," I said, which wasn't exactly the truth. "You'll have to land him yourself."

Joey squirmed in his seat from side to side as the pike ran back and forth around the bow. I dipped the net into the water. When the fish came alongside of us, I slipped the net under a 40-inch northern.

"I caught one!" Joey shouted.

"You sure did," I said.

"And with nobody's help!"

I recognized the smile on Joey's face. At last he had beaten bad luck. I also knew that in the years ahead, no matter what else might occur, he would always remember this day in the Rainbow Woods when he did the impossible and—all by himself—caught a giant pike that should have got away.

There are other lakes in the Rainbow Woods where I visit yesterday. Here, where time is fixed, the past is never far away.

FOUR

Promises to Keep

On the coldest nights of winter, when the mercury plummets and snowdrifts as tall as horses winnow in the wind, you'll find me on the frozen Nemadji River, about a mile upstream of Lake Superior. Look for the light of my lantern.

I use a spud to chop away ice from the hole I fished the night before. Then I sit on an overturned bucket, jigging a Doctor spoon or shiner, placing the lantern next to the hole so that its light can keep me warm—if that's possible. Although I'm swaddled in Thinsulate from my pate to my toes, I may be wrapped in an old army blanket, too. Tonight the wind chill factor was ten below zero—cold enough to keep the riffraff indoors. The murderous elements assure me of privacy; then again, few people fish for burbot.

The burbot isn't a game fish. It resembles an eel and fights like an anchor, but the burbot from Lake Superior are as tasty as cod. They dwell in the lake's icy, unplumbed depths, too deep to be caught by summer anglers. But once a year, for a few weeks in midwinter, the fish move into rivers at night to spawn. One of these is the Nemadji, which lies within sight of my house. Here, under the ice, burbot mix their eggs and milt.

Tonight I caught three fish, each as big as an average pike. I'm not a huge fan of burbot, but I'd rather be fishing than dreaming about it. This is especially true during the long winters of the Lake Superior country, where the sun drops behind the trees by four in the afternoon. If I want to go fishing when the day's work is done, I'm pretty much limited to jigging for burbot in the dark. And I do want to fish because I have promises to keep.

* * *

Like the oldest kid in any large family (and in our family there were ten), I grew up shouldering responsibilities I never thought about—unless they got in the way of fishing. I missed a lot of white bass runs peddling newspapers or helping Dad with yard-work; the perch seemed to bite best whenever I'd walk my lolly-gagging little sisters home from school. I didn't mind this sort of thing because I knew it was expected of me; I also knew that someday, when I was older, I would fish whenever I wanted. It was a promise that I made to myself at twelve, and that I regularly renewed well into my forties.

To be sure, life changes with age. After college there's a career and then marriage and children. I was sure my life would be different, but it wasn't. I passed up Saturday outings to nearby streams because I was busy. I'd plan and then cancel fishing trips to distant places, hoping next year I could swing it without shorting the tooth fairy. When the steelhead were running, my in-laws would fly into town for a visit; when salmon were spawning, I was cheering my son at his high school football games. If I did have a free day for fishing it would rain, or be too windy, or sometimes even snow.

I don't regret all the hours I missed on lakes and streams attending to family, but I do chastise the man in my shaving mirror whenever I think of all the times he *could* have gone fishing, but didn't. What if it was too wet, too cold, too late, or too dark? You can't wait for perfect timing if you want to fish—or if you want a life instead of promises. Promises keep us going when the going gets rough, but sometimes promises become substitutes for the real thing. There's a quote from Voltaire that should be emblazoned above the place where every angler hangs his gear: "We never live; we are always in the expectation of living." Life is what happens while we're making other plans. We live, seldom aware of being alive. Like the migration of burbot beneath the ice of a winter stream, life proceeds unnoticed. And largely untried.

* * *

Nowadays—grizzled, gouty, and gerontic—I still make plans and occasionally get away to fish distant places. But I've also taken to fishing my home waters whenever I can, even if it's only for an hour or two at the end of the day. I fish for burbot for the same reason I dip-net for ciscoes in the early dark of November evenings, and seine for smelt beneath April's brilliant stars. It's why I leave the supper table on summer evenings to battle tiny bluegills in a nearby pond, or walk to a stream where the brookies are barely bigger than my thumb.

It's not the fish but the *fishing* that matters. It's not the time we have, but how we use it that counts. It's not the life we plan to live, but what we do with the one we're given that will make the difference when seasons end, and rods and reels know only dust.

The boy to whom I promised so much isn't getting any younger. That's why on the coldest nights of winter, when temperatures plummet and snow drifts winnow in the wind, you'll find me on the frozen Nemadji. It's where I'm keeping some promises I made to a small boy, long ago. Look for the light of our lantern.

FIVE

The Lonely Land

The Blue Hills were once a great mountain range that dominated their landscape. Formed by lava more than a billion years ago when the earth's crust was torn asunder, they would have dwarfed the Alps we know today. But innumerable eons of winds and rains, immersion in Paleozoic seas, and erosion by ancient glaciers have reduced them to a chain of softly sculpted hills high above Wisconsin's Chippewa River. Shrouded in a smoky, blue haze, they loom against the skyline like a lonely land.

There are no towns in the Blue Hills and only a few washboard roads. Ghost towns and abandoned farms lie hidden among the hollows. The isolation deepens in deep ravines furrowed with swift creeks. Here, where people seldom wander, the fishing is still as good as it used to be.

I first saw the hills years ago on a visit to Gundy's Canyon. In those days Old Man Gunderson would hitch his horses to a rickety hay wagon and tote a load of Boy Scouts, fishermen, or whoever else wanted to come along down a narrow trail between the canyon's sheer walls. Set in the center of a glacial moraine, the canyon is among the deepest in the North. Rugged, rocky, and 125 feet deep, the chasm was reminiscent of a misty, mountain gorge.

The highlight of the trip was Hell's Hole. Here a trout stream plummeted from the canyon's rim, only to vanish into a hole in the ground before suddenly reappearing some distance away. The canyon's floor was marked with mysterious stone cairns, mounds of chipped rocks gathered into neat piles. Some said they were left behind by Indian arrowhead makers; others claimed the cairns were the devil's work from the night before. As a boy, sitting around the campfire at night and listening to spooky stories as shadows prowled the black timber, the Blue Hills were a place as otherworldly as the ghosts they concealed.

Not long ago I visited the hills again. My excuse for a visit was the opening day of trout season, but more than this I wanted to see if the hills were as I recalled, if anything about them had changed, and if their mysteries were still as arcane. I started out one morning from Weyerhauser, a tiny town at the southern edge of the hills, named for the nineteenth-century timber baron. It was here where Frederick Weyerhauser made his first fortune: nowhere else in the world did white pines grow as thick and tall.

More than once, I passed the cavities of decaying stumps that measured four feet across. Most of the stumps were blackened with char, evidence of the wildfires that swept the hills when the pines were leveled and the loggers pulled out. Fires devastated the valleys but the ridges escaped, unscathed. Today, mature hardwoods blanket the hilltops while the hollows are a tangle of brush. Only a few of the old growth, virgin pines remain, the last survivors of a vanishing tribe.

I followed the only road heading north out of Weyerhauser to where a trail skirted Devil's Creek into a rough and roadless area. I made a few casts for the stream's speckled trout, landing a pair of brookies that were as dark and wild as moccasin flowers. I climbed out of the stream's gorge and followed the spine of an esker before dropping down into a valley where beavers were at work. Here I took another brookie on a worm—a speckled squaretail that was all of a pound. Further on, I came across a tiny, bog-encircled lake, rimmed with tamaracks; the heather quaked with my every step. At its edge, I peered down into an amber-colored lake as clear as iced tea. Largemouth bass cruised along the edge of the heather.

Although the tide of spring migration was past, the country was teeming with birds. Cedar waxwings whistled among the bog's larches, where chickadees and nuthatches were at work. At one lake I found loons and then, further down the trail, I caught the rasping squeal of a red-tail hawk, high against the blue. Here, too, the trailside woods were filled with the warbling of purple finches, the *jee-jee-jee* of crossbills, and the canary-like call of a goldfinch.

Occasionally, I passed the wreck of an abandoned farm. The Scandinavian immigrants who tried to create homesteads from the loggers' ruin reaped nothing but disappointment from a land that yielded only slash. Families who weren't burned out by wildfires lost everything to the Great Depression. By 1950, the year I was born, the Blue Hills were once again a wilderness.

I stopped to eat my lunch where Hemlock Creek crossed a dirt road. I sat on the bridge, eating a sandwich and apple, watching brook trout dart in a stream where it was possible no one had cast a line in several seasons. The water was quick, icy clear, and filled with native fish—the brook trout I took here were as big as jumbo perch. I spent a couple of hours at the bridge, expecting other fishermen to arrive, but the solitudes of the Blue Hills and Hemlock Creek remained unbroken.

Upstream of the bridge lay the ruins of an old dam and campground. At one time the dam held back the waters of sprawling Murphy Lake, but flash floods years ago washed out the dam and drained the flowage. The same thing occurred at nearby Bolger

Flowage and Bucks Lake. Bucks Lake was eventually restored, but Murphy and Bolger lakes remained phantoms.

There was something sad about the old campground at Murphy Lake. Its roads were washed out, its campsites overgrown, and it was clear no one had visited the place in years. A porcupine was gnawing at the sill logs of a rotting shed, and in a place where people once gathered to enjoy the warmth of campfires and friends, I found only the dried and decaying haunch of a deer. Spring was unfolding, streams were flush with trout, and anywhere else waterways would have been populated by opening day anglers. But the streams of the Blue Hills lay neglected, as lost and forgotten as a discarded dream.

* * *

Violent storms regularly sweep the Blue Hills, causing creeks to flood and roads to vanish. Winds topple huge stands of timber, blocking trails and sealing off entire chasms with their trout streams. Many of these secluded areas remain isolated for years, and one of these was now Gundy's Canyon: the entrance was sealed shut by a solid dam of timber that fell in a storm, long ago.

"Nobody's visited that canyon in years," said the clerk at the gas station in Weyerhauser.

Nevertheless, I headed out to the canyon but was stopped by the locked gate at Gunderson's farm. The old man had died, and like other farms among the hills his place stood vacant and deserted. The paint was all but gone from a weathered sign beside the road; it took a bit of imagination to read the words: "Gundy's Canyon." I thought about that chasm, the wonder of Hell's Hole, and the mysterious, stone cairns—all of it lost to view for years to come.

But to the Blue Hills, nothing was different. To them—which had watched an infant earth be ripped asunder, seen the ebb and flow of Paleozoic seas, and felt the crushing weight of ancient glaciers—nothing was more inconsequential than one man's yearning to visit a canyon stream. I looked at the faded sign beside the road, and once again felt the press of otherworldliness. Men are mortal, passing, and fleet, but the Blue Hills stand in the lonely land of eternity.

SIX

The November Season

You know November has arrived when lakes begin to freeze and naked aspens stand stark and gray. Now, for a little while, the Lake Superior country lies abandoned, as alone and unvisited as it used to be. Autumn is ending and most fishermen have vanished; lonely streams pass unnoticed beneath leaden skies and the distant, high tolling of geese. Life is changing as autumn slips away. Everything is ready for the coming of the snow.

Here, where water is fixed in ice for almost six months of the year, November signals the end of fishing. Ahead lie long months of frozen lakes and streams, killing cold, and snowbound landscapes. Those of us who can have already fled south to warmer climes. The rest of us spend autumn's final hours on our local streams, hoping to land one more fish before winter arrives and puts an end to things.

It was that way for me the day I visited the White River, not far from where the stream meets the Bad River east of Chequamegon Bay. I came to the river in a rush, my mind filled with the things I had done and the things I needed to do before I was ready for winter. There was firewood to cut, tires to change, windows to winterize, and the snow-blower needed overhauling.

I hit the water and began fishing as though I were in a race; but all urgency vanished when the first fish struck.

It took the spinner as soon as the Rooster Tail fell among the black spruce sweepers; from the start, I knew I was into one of the White's real trout. The fish ran upstream and down before it tired enough for me to land it—a 3-pound brown with a hooked jaw, luminous with flecks of vermilion, and as dark as the spruces that shadowed its pool.

I released the fish, lit a cigarette, and sat down on a log, waiting for the shakes to pass. The silence and sense of isolation were profound. Gone were the rustlings of small animals and the calling of birds; gone, too, were other anglers. Grouse hunters had given up, deer hunters had yet to arrive, and no one was waiting for me at a rendezvous downstream. Concern slipped away like snakeskin as I slowly settled into the untroubled rhythm of November. For the first time in a long time, I felt no compunction to be somewhere else, doing what anxiety demanded.

* * *

Two days later I was fishing the salmon streams that hurry north to Lake Superior, on either side of the Middle River. The runs on these sandstone streams aren't what they used to be, but the salmon still return—cohos, mostly, but also a few chinooks. Often the fish turn up in unexpected places: I once landed a 6-pound chinook while fishing for brook trout on a creek so narrow I could spit across it.

The water was low and as clear as amber in the Amnicon. I followed an old trail around a series of waterfalls, dry birch leaves crackling like parchment beneath my feet. Frozen puddles pockmarked the clay path, and for the first time it was cold enough to wear gloves. Buffleheads burst from a pool as I climbed down into a sandstone canyon. Through the spray and mist, I saw a fish hurl itself up and over the lower falls. The salmon runs on these small streams are not as spectacular as other places, but they are important to those of us who winter over in the North. Because of this I return to the streams until deep snows make them inaccessible, even though the runs peak in early autumn.

I come not only for the cohos and chinooks, but also for the rugged beauty of sandstone canyons, the unrestrained thunder of waterfalls, and the sight of salmon leaping rock ledges like timber wolves hurdling windfalls. Here, in November, the wild is always calling.

* * *

Just before Thanksgiving I wandered up the Bois Brule to Rainbow Bend. Stretches of the stream were already sealed in ice, and ten inches of snow lay along the banks. It was clear no one else had recently ventured near the river.

The Brule and I have a ritual that we have observed for decades: in April and May I come for the spring run of steelhead, followed by brookies in June, brown trout throughout the summer, and salmon when the maples turn red. In November I return for the autumn run of rainbows. These autumn-run steelhead winter over in the stream before migrating back to Lake Superior in the spring.

To be sure, the best fishing is long past by November; like most of the steelhead streams at the head of the Great Lakes, the run peaks in October. By November, most fish have moved upstream past the point where fishing is allowed. But that still leaves several weeks of open water—and that means everything to a northern angler. Then, too, you have the river to yourself in

November, so you can do the sort of mental accounting that fishermen engage in as each year ends.

How many fish had I caught since April? How many did I lose? How many times could I have gone fishing, but didn't?

Six or seven months of open water is not enough time for all the fishing I hope to do each year. Maybe it's because I'm better at making plans than acting on them, or because I feel guilty about fishing when I should be mowing the lawn, or because a rainy weekend makes a fine excuse to stick close to the TV, or because I still believe I have a limitless store of tomorrows. And although I firmly resolve every January to do more fishing in the coming year, November finds me casting a line as often as I can in a frantic attempt to salvage my good intentions. In the North, in November, winter can arrive on any day and put an end to fishing.

It was snowing by the time I made Tickle Run—soft, white, crystalline flakes that obliterated the Brule's landmarks and that piled up quickly in winnowing drifts on frozen patches of the stream. Down they came, a wintry cascade of snow, accentuating November's silence and seclusion.

I pulled my hood over my head. Snow was collecting in the creases of my coat; even in neoprene, the press of icy water made my legs ache. The season was over. Winter was here. Within hours, snow would seal shut the country and it would be April before I was free to fish open water again. I had hoped to catch one more fish, but if I didn't leave soon I'd run the risk of getting stuck in the snow. I took a final, deliberate cast and then headed downstream.

At the swinging bridge, I stopped to say goodbye to the river. Ice was forming a lid over the flatwater beneath the span—and if the fish hadn't darted just then, I would have missed it. But there it was, nose pointed upstream, silver and bright amid the encircling gloom, a 30-inch steelhead holding itself steady at the edge of the current in the lambent pool below the bridge. And then—with a single, powerful flick of its tail—it vanished upstream beneath the ice.

But the sight of it was enough, and the dazzling image would keep me company through winter's beleaguering days. Knowing it was there, waiting beneath the ice for spring's return, was reason enough to dream about April and the new year of fishing it would bring.

I took a final look at the river, said goodbye, and headed back downstream. Winter had arrived and snow was falling all around me, but while it had lasted I'd made the most of November.

SEVEN

The End of the Trail

The Gunflint Trail is part of the wilderness lakes and rivers, the rocky portages and far horizons, and the wide, uncluttered solitudes of the Quetico-Superior country.

It looks much like any other road where it starts in the small town of Grand Marais, Minnesota. From there, it rolls away like a bituminous river to the northwest, through a rugged and little-populated land, before ending in a cul-de-sac near big Saganaga Lake, sixty miles away. En route, the trail passes a score of wilderness lakes where moose come to feed, loons call unheard, and fish seldom see a lure. But the real jewel of this wilderness road lies at the end of the trail itself, where the blue, vast expanse of Saganaga Lake sweeps far away to the north. This is the place where all roads end, and where the fabled lands of the Saganagons and Kawnipi begin. Here, where the wild has yet to be disturbed, travel is still a matter of packs, paddles, and canoes.

The first time I saw the Gunflint was late in the year, after the first snows had fallen and its lakes lay bound in ice. I was traveling with friends, exploring the country between the Brule and Greenwood rivers, and one night we visited a lake within earshot of the trail.

The temperature hovered somewhere near zero, and in the icy-clear weather the stars seemed bright enough to cast shadows. Owls called from the black spruce forest, while shifting shapes moved soundlessly against the darkening shore. Suddenly we saw them: a line of gray, mute ghosts, moving single file across the ice at the far end of the lake, tails high in the air and trotting over the snow in the way only timber wolves can move.

In that same instant the sky was split by a bright gash, and in the next moment the night was aglow with the shining ribbons of the aurora. The gleaming streamers fell from the sky like water plunging from a falls; and when the wolves began to call, the northern lights throbbed with their howling. From that moment on, the Gunflint Trail was something more than just a road for me.

It has always been part of the area known as the Arrowhead Region. In the old days, it was the winter route of Indians, traders, and prospectors, and now it serves as a main access road to the Boundary Waters Canoe Area Wilderness. Most of it parallels the Voyageurs' Highway: the network of lakes and rivers that make up the American–Canadian border and that served as a major fur-trading route until the mid-nineteenth century. Traders for the Hudson Bay, Northwest, and American Fur companies traveled this waterway for 200 years, and the portages they marked between the border lakes are still visible and used by travelers today.

Among my favorite lakes along the trail is Northern Light Lake. Part of Minnesota's Brule River, the lake is a long stretch of flatwater, pretty and pristine as any in the North. Despite its easy accessibility from the trail, it has the look of the primeval, and once on the water the world of roads and towns feels far away.

One time, just as it was getting dark, I came around a point in the twilight and surprised a moose standing in the shallows of a weedy bay. It was a mature bull with a rack far wider than my canoe, and I prepared myself for the worst. I turned in the water, bracing for the violent turbulence that would come when the animal bolted. But nothing like that happened. Instead, the moose simply lifted its head, watching as I silently glided past his dark presence, before turning his attention back to the weeds.

Another time, some friends and I camped at Flour Lake. We had come to see the huge virgin pines for which the lake is famous, as well as for Flour's walleye fishing. One evening I made the half-mile trek to the top of Honeymoon Bluff. The lookout point is a bare ledge of glaciated rock, high above the surrounding country, with an overlook of Hungry Jack Lake and endless miles of wilderness. It was quiet on top of the bluff, so soundless that the hum of insects was like a dull roar. The sunset's last rays had cast the woods with a golden light, while the lake below glittered like sparkling wine.

I looked out across Hungry Jack and the gilded hills beyond. A single canoe was moving across the water, but from that height it was smaller than a matchstick. I watched the canoe as it moved north toward West Bearskin Lake, wondering how far it would travel. Beyond West Bearskin lay Duncan Lake and the Stairway Portage, and beyond that was big Rose, a main link in the voyageurs' old route. From there, the possibilities of where a canoe might go were infinite. For all I knew, the canoe on Hungry Jack might be on its way to Hudson Bay, or be setting out along the old trade route to Lake Athabasca, more than a thousand miles away in the far northwest. Down there, near the end of the trail on Hungry Jack Lake, a man in a canoe was as free as any person could be.

Suddenly I wanted to be down there on Hungry Jack, paddling my own canoe into the distance. I wanted to know what lay beyond those gilded hills; I wanted to feel the thrill of seeing a place that until the moment of discovery had existed only in a dream. But then the sun disappeared, the woods turned black, and both the canoe and Hungry Jack were lost to the valley's darkness; and I was left standing on Honeymoon Bluff, alone with my thoughts and longings.

* * *

Another time in the last days of summer, I pitched a tent at Seagull Lake and spent most of a week roaming the woods and waterways at the very end of the trail. Early in the mornings, in the deep places below the tall granite bluffs that rise above Seagull, I caught smallmouths for breakfast while flocks of black ducks passed overhead. In the afternoons, I watched bears comb for berries on the fire-scarred bank of the Gull River, or I took long walks along lonely forest trails. There was always something to see: the approach of a storm; the antics of chipmunks; the arrival of people coming out of the wilderness after days of travel, eager to share their tales with me. I was happy and should have been content; yet, at night when I studied my maps, the big, blue expanse of Saganaga Lake lying just north of my camp kept calling me.

In the end, the need to know those unseen distances became more important than anything else. I obtained the necessary permits and, early one morning, shoved off in my canoe for Saganaga.

I paddled north, beyond the trail and through the waist of a narrows, moving out of a bay with the sun at my back until the wide breadth of Saganaga lay before me like a sea. In the distance its legions of rocky islands were like fleets of anchored ships, and at the sight of them I felt myself being swept up in the big lake's unchanging lure.

Strange stirrings tug at a man when he looks upon a natural wonder as immense and wild as Saganaga. His mind races with dreams of exploration, and of visiting places no one else has seen. It's the feeling Hennepin must have had in discovering Niagara Falls, and what John Colter experienced in traveling the unexplored Yellowstone.

In most places today it is almost impossible to recapture the impressions of those early frontiersman, but sprawling Saganaga Lake remains much as it always has. Its forested shores and rocky islands are still remote; its long, blue distances still exceed the limits of vision; its loons still call, its waves still crash against its rocks, and its solitudes and silences remain vast.

I looked down at my map and saw the great, roadless area lying northwest of the big lake: places like the Saganagons, the Kawnipi, Batchewaung Lake and beyond. The country rolled away unbroken to the borders of the map, and what the paper could not hold filled my imagination.

In that moment, the distant headlands of Saganaga tugged at me with their unrelenting pull. It was the wilderness calling me forward, beckoning me to leave the road behind and to venture on in my canoe. I looked down the long channel between the islands, and for a moment I almost succumbed. But then the loons began to call, the noon light began to fade, and I realized I would have to hurry to make Seagull Lake before dark. I took a last look across Saganaga and turned toward camp.

But I was already making plans to return, for the end of the Gunflint Trail is only a beginning. The roadless country beyond it was calling, waiting to be explored, and until I returned it would give me no rest.

EIGHT

The Everlasting

Now that I'm gray, balding, and thoroughly middle-aged, I think I know why my father so enjoyed wading for walleyes. It had to do with the easy familiarity of little streams and the everlasting joy of fishing.

In those days we fished the St. Croix River near its headwaters in northwestern Wisconsin. Here the bourbon-colored stream was barely 20 yards wide. We didn't need an expensive boat or pricey gadgets to fish it. A pair of hip boots, a long light spinning rod, and a few jigs and night crawlers were all we required. Simplicity let us get close to the stream and know it in a way that complexity never allows.

My memory is filled with the image of otters playing like children, the fragrance of cedars, and the cold press of water against my shins. I can still hear the *swoosh* of my father's 7-foot rod slice the evening's hush as he cast a leadhead jig into the back eddy below the rapids. Then there was that long, hesitant moment before he lifted the rod's tip and retrieved the jig back with the current.

"Got one!"

I still think stream walleyes are better battlers than those caught in lakes. Maybe it's because they use the current as a buckler, or because they're caught in shallow water. What I do know is that in all the years Dad and I fished walleyes along little streams like the upper St. Croix, we never once came across another angler.

Back then, most walleye fishermen were already seeking out big, popular, and heavily fished rivers where boats formed a constant flotilla from April through August. Others fished well-known lakes, coming home empty-handed whenever summer weather turned unseasonably sizzling or cold. But my father and I always caught fish.

Dad never fished for walleyes until the gloaming—that quiet time that comes at the end of the day. He claimed that walleyes could see better after sunset and schooled wherever the river provided a place for ambush. Our favorite place on the river was just downstream of its source in Lac St. Croix. Here, near the shallow head of a rocky pool, walleyes waited at dusk with their noses pointed upstream, ready to snatch whatever the quickwater brought them. One evening a fish struck my jig on the first cast. In an instant, I knew I had tied into one of the St. Croix's lunker walleyes.

"Looks like a big one!" Dad shouted. "Don't let it get away!" He was on the bank, jumping up and down like a jack-in-a-box.

Later, when I got the fish up on the bank and Dad held the lantern over it, we saw a walleye that was all of 4 pounds. To me, the fish was a monster.

"Nice one," said Dad. His soft voice was barely audible above the hissing Coleman lantern; yet, after all this time, I can still hear him.

* * *

Nowadays, on summer evenings, I wade walleye streams whenever my longing for yesterday is more than I can bear. Usually it happens when I'm made aware of how complex life has become, and of the enormous toll it exacts from a man's enthusiasm. Then, like a wounded deer seeking thick cover, I retreat to the St. Croix.

Like my father, I fish for walleyes at the gloaming, when winds vanish, whippoorwills call, and the twilight resounds with the whine of insects. Nighthawks swoop and bats flutter like fairies over the water. You can almost feel the dusk exert its calm. I fish the gloaming more often than I used to.

Nowadays my teenage son and I stand by the car and bathe in insect repellent before striking out for the banks of the St. Croix. We work our way upstream, slowly and purposefully, making each cast count, aware that time is short and the fishing always ends too soon. Nick pays special attention to submerged trees and logs, the tail end of deep pools, and the water below rapids and tributaries. Like me, he has developed an intimacy with the stream and knows each of these places as well as he does his own backyard.

In the last level rays of sunlight, we come to the place where my father and I fished years ago. Nick and I make a few dozen casts and catch several walleyes, none of them keepers. I remove my leadhead jig and replace it with a soft-body floating model, tipping the hook with a night crawler. Above this, I pinch a piece of split shot.

Again I cast to the shallow head of the pool, keeping the rod tip up to better feel the weight bounce along the bottom before it suddenly stops. I reel in the slack line and set the rod in the crotch of a forked stick shoved into the bank. My father called this "dummy fishing." I call it a reprieve. This is the only time and place where I can do nothing and still feel that I'm accomplishing my grand schemes.

I sit on the bank and watch the past. It floats by like smoke on the water. The sun has set and a fiery magenta sky blazes with the afterglow. The flatwater is red. Overhead, wood ducks whistle. A beaver swims past me, oblivious of my presence. All this is as familiar to me as a room in which I spent a lot of time, long ago. Here is a calm and constancy that quickly soothes my psyche.

"Got one!"

Nick is calling, and one look is enough to tell me he's tied into something big. The fish is using the current to its advantage, and the light spinning rod bends like a willow switch. I scramble down the bank, wanting to help. For an instant, I wonder if Nick will land the fish. But by the time I reach him, Nick is threading a stringer under the gill cover of a 4-pound walleye.

"Nice fish," I tell him.

The lantern I'm holding illuminates more than my son's smile. Like an old song that stirs a memory, the hissing lantern reminds me of the past. I think of my own father and wish he were here. Meanwhile, Nick is wading back into the St. Croix.

"Bet I catch another!" he calls.

To be sure, rivers change as much as people. Time erodes and alters all things. Only the joy of fishing is everlasting—that, and the memories it makes.

PART TWO

FORESTS AND FIELDS

NINE

The Solitude Hunter

Years ago, as a boy, I found a cure for things whenever life began to crowd me. I'd pocket a few shotshells, pick up the .410, and light out, alone, for the woods.

My search for space always ended in a stand of old oaks along Wisconsin's upper Fox River. A hundred years earlier that country had been the wilderness haunt of John Muir, but by the time I inherited it the great forest was gone and my oaks were little more than a woodlot. Still, something of the old wilderness remained in the ancient trees, and I spent many autumn afternoons alone among them. But although I filled many game bags in those woods, I never thought of that place in terms of spent shot and squirrel tails.

Despite the fact that I was only a boy and knew nothing of a man's need to spend time alone in the wild places, the longing and hunger were still there. In the fragile silence of the oaks, I found the solitude for which I searched: I took to it as naturally as a bird takes to air.

That was many years ago, and plenty of things have changed. But in the fall, whenever life comes to push-and-shove again, the cure is still the same.

* * *

Nowadays, when gray winds begin to blow and the first aspen leaves turn tawny-gold, I pack a few things and head for Wisconsin's Nicolet Forest. Others hunters work this area at the same time as I do, but seldom have I come across so much as another man's bootprint. One reason is that I prefer the lowly stream bottoms others ignore. These are the small, near-nameless tributaries of rivers like the Popple, the Pine, the Oconto, and the Pike. Usually the banks are overgrown in alders and hazelbrush, and even a slow walk through the thickets can be an ordeal. If I'm lucky, I'll kick up grouse and woodcock, or perhaps flush a pair of wood ducks. But my real quest is for those things that will never fill a game bag: the sight of a doe silently feeding beside a forest pool; a pileated woodpecker jackhammering the stub of an ash; the last purple spike of pickerelweed in bloom beside a stream bank; the unmistakable "woof" of a bear if I've wandered too deep into the hawthorns.

Once, while following an old logging trail near the Archibald Lakes, I came across a stand of trees known as the Cathedral Pines. These were the trees the Indians knew, the last of a lost and almost-vanished world. The tops of the great trees disappeared in a dark canopy that the sun had not penetrated in years. Below, in a world of perpetual twilight, the ground was thick and soft with rusty needles that had been accumulating there for untold centuries.

The survival of the Cathedral Pines was a marvel in itself. They had escaped loggers, wildfires, windstorms, and disease, and though some people claimed that the preservation of the ancient pines was a waste of valuable timber, the real value of the trees could not be measured in board feet. Nor would the pines long interest a hunter who was only intent on bagging game.

There was no sign of deer, grouse, squirrels, or rabbits—the trees were too old and large to provide cover and food. Instead, the significance of the Cathedral Pines was their quality of transcendence. Wherever one of the giants had fallen, sunlight streamed through the resulting hole in the forest canopy, illuminating the earth. There, in a slanted shaft of sunlight, the ageless dust of space floated through the trees.

On another occasion I was visiting friends in a large Midwestern city, when suddenly I felt the need to escape the crowds and to get away to a quiet place. One afternoon, while my friends were away at work, I packed my host's 20-gauge and a fistful of shotshells, slipped out of his apartment, and drove to a marsh that lay almost within the shadow of the city's skyline.

I spent the afternoon beating the swales and canary grass, going through the motions of hunting pheasants. I kicked up two, young roosters but for one reason or another I never fired a shot. Perhaps it was because I had no dog and feared that any bird I might drop would never be found. More likely, however, was that the birds were only an excuse to get away from the city and spend time outdoors.

That evening, as other hunters were packing up and leaving, I climbed a knoll above the marsh and had a smoke. Shooting hours were over, and the men and their guns would be gone until another sunrise. Alone now, I would have the marsh to myself.

The sun fell away as the moon began to rise, and somewhere in the swale a lone coyote called to the approaching night. The sky faded to the cloudy color of an old gun barrel in need of bluing, while a faraway skein of Canada geese filled the air with their heartbreaking cries. Two sandhill cranes dropped out of the sky, like pterodactyls from another time; in the fading light, the croak of their primitive calls rolled across the marsh like an echo from an ancient world. For a moment, I thought I caught a glimpse of what Earth had been like when men were more like beasts, huddling in caves against the night. And as the evening mists rose and billowed across the marsh, I had the feeling as though I were peering through the mists of time.

Forty miles away was a city and its suburbs of more than a million people: a helter-skelter world of hustle and hype. But that evening, sitting alone on the knoll with the empty gun across my lap, the gulf between me and that city was more than one of mere miles.

In such experiences and impressions lie the reasons for hunting, for the answer as to why a man picks up a gun and enters the woods each fall will never be found in the number of birds bagged or in the count of points on a deer's rack. After all the wordy arguments and psychoanalytic discussions, the truth about hunting remains the same: it is not so much a blood sport, as it is a ritual of spirit. This is the reason why men choose to hunt, often times alone; for it is in those moments as a solitary hunter that man makes contact with a world and way of life that remains indelibly etched in his soul.

* * *

I found that world late one November while hunting alone in a roadless area west of Port Wing on Lake Superior. It was the last day of deer season and although it was only three in the afternoon, the sun was already beginning to set behind the spruces and balsams.

Just before dark, I startled a buck in a balsam thicket below a ridgetop. But before I could raise my .30-30 for a shot, the deer's white flag disappeared downhill into a cedar swamp. Although it was dusk and camp lay four miles away through the snowy woods, I decided to follow the buck down into the cedars.

The already icy temperatures began to drop, the wind disappeared, and beyond the cedars a frozen stream lay soundless, gray, and flat. Stars appeared in the sky and I knew that even if I jumped the deer again, it would be too dark for a shot. But it was the last hour of the season, and I wanted to make things last. I wanted the buck, but even more, I wanted the awareness of hunting, of stalking him through the silent, winnowing drifts of fresh snow, alone in the wild solitudes of wilderness.

At the river bottom I found where the buck had crossed to the other side of the stream. It was senseless to follow any farther, and my heart ached at the thought. Still, there would be the long walk back to camp along the river, and for a little while longer I could have the silences of the woods to myself.

Now the sky was flooded with moonlight and stars, and beneath them the snow-shrouded stream lay dazzling. An owl called and I saw a snowshoe hare jump for the cover of a balsam bough; a white weasel bounded across a snowy log for the far side of the stream, silent, swift, and deadly. Night was quickly coming on, and with the darkness every killing thing began to stalk the woods.

I walked up the windswept, frozen stream at an easy pace, the surface clean and immaculate. I listened to the ice groan with the deepening freeze, and the sound of unseen animals moving along the banks in the darkness. Alone and miles away from the nearest human being, I was glad to have decided to stay out past sundown, walking back to camp along the river, through the moonlit, wintry solitudes.

Ten minutes later the first timber wolf howled.

It was somewhere up on the ridge, off to my right; but my imagination began seeing wolves in every shadow along the cedar-clad banks. I knew I had nothing to fear; I knew it was unlikely timber wolves would attack a man; I knew all the old horror stories were just tales and myths. I knew all this—but in that moment, I didn't believe a word of it.

The howl came again, closer now—a lonesome, mournful keening. Instantly it was answered by a second wolf's cry, and then I heard the sound of them moving through the brush, down the ridge toward the river. The woods along the bank cracked and crashed as the animals jumped over logs and windfalls. Whenever they did the fear in me would swell.

I hurried along the river, the wolves paralleling me. Up ahead, the stream quickly narrowed between the rock walls of a rapids. I would have to crawl up the steep bank on hands and knees to circumnavigate the open water. When I did, I'd be off-balance and helpless: it would be the perfect place and time for the wolves to attack. Involuntarily, I clutched my rifle tighter.

Thirty feet from the narrows I stopped, stone-still. Years passed as I waited, trying to decide whether to trust in what I knew or in my instinctual dread. Then I heard something crash as the wolves moved upstream of the open water. I knew then that if I had ever been in danger, the threat was now past. I sighed with relief. Only then did I notice that I was trembling.

Later, when I heard the wolves howl again, the cry came from a place far away; and later still, when I heard the final wail, it seemed to come to me from across miles of time and space.

I had been frightened by the wolves, but also exhilarated. Hearing their call had been a kind of testament to the wildness of that country, and to the things I sought as a solitude hunter—things like wild places where the calling of timber wolves still lingers, and where a lone and solitary hunter can still bridge the gap between the present and primordial—between the world of rocks and trees and stars and dust, and the often artificial, spiritless press of modern life.

* * *

Years ago, as a boy, I found a cure for things whenever life began to crowd me. I'd pocket a few shotshells, pick up the gun, and light out, alone, for the woods. Much time has passed since then, and my life is different in many ways. But after all these years and their changes, the remedy is still the same.

TEN

Keeper of the Flame

In Wisconsin, deer camps are a family tradition and each one has its history. For as long as I can remember, every member of our family old enough to hunt was expected to show up at my father's camp on the eve of opening day. Dad always served squirrel stew that first evening, and as we ate he'd tell about the big buck he'd seen while coming into camp. His thoughts on where we should hunt in the morning weren't suggestions—they were *commands*. But only the youngest of us resented his decrees; after all, Dad was the patriarch of deer camp.

But this year things are different. This year, Dad has passed the banner to me. Now it is my turn to be the tender of tradition, and the new curator of our deer camp's history.

My own son is still too young to hunt, so my gray-haired father-in-law, Robert—the lone, surviving elder of our camp—drove up with me to open the cabin and to personally bestow the emblems of my new position: Dad's huge stew kettle and a thawing package of squirrels. I think both Dad and Robert want to make sure I don't tamper with things. But already I've jeopardized tradition—I forgot the cribbage board.

"We always play cribbage in deer camp," Robert reminds me.

"We can play poker," I say.

"No, we can't. It's not the same."

Robert is nice enough not to say anything about it, but I know he has never trusted me to do things the right way—which is, of course, the way that he and my father did it, and the way their fathers did it before that. Robert doesn't trust the red potatoes I bought for the stew ("White ones taste better," he claims), the sharpness of my paring knife, or the popple logs I'm burning in the wood stove. "We always used oak," Robert says.

Together we peel potatoes and onions, and cut up the six squirrels. They are fox squirrels with heavy hams and thick saddles, and three of them would be more than enough to make stew. But Robert insists on using all six. "That's the way it's done," he says.

Nor is the way I'm slicing onions quite suitable for this nitpicking old man. "*Dice* them," he says; then, in a fit of exasperation, he takes the knife and dices them himself. I fill the stew kettle with water and set it on the stove. Not quite enough water for Robert. He suggests I add more.

I have hunted with Robert since I was a boy. I'm now as old as he was when I married his daughter, whom I've taken good care of for many years. Yet Robert makes me feel like a child again, and not a very bright one at that. But there is no resentment on my part—only a warmth in knowing that this old man will forever think of me as a kid.

I look out the window at the coming dark. It's growing late and the first inch of tracking snow is filling the woods. Time passes quickly, and so, too, do generations. I sneak a peek at Robert—white-whiskered, stoop-shouldered, joints aching with old wounds. He is our camp's only tribal elder, but one day—too soon—I will join those ranks.

"I wish Dad was here," I say. It sounds like something I might have said the first time I shot a deer, and then walked up to the dead animal, alone and wondering what to do. Robert remembers that day. He looks up from the wood stove where the squirrel stew is bubbling and—for the first time in a long time—really looks at me. Nothing is said, but something has passed between us. A bridge has been crossed. For both of us, there is no going back.

Adulthood arrives in these quiet, little ways until the torch is finally passed to us by an elder; then we become the keeper of the flame, the steward of the clan, the guardian of tradition. We become the patriarchs of deer camps, duck blinds, and fishing shacks. It becomes our turn to make a place where friends and family are always welcomed, to share in days afield that are largely our invention and where tradition is either relayed or repealed, depending upon our dispositions.

* * *

A pickup truck pulls up to the cabin; Steve and Mike have arrived. They, too, are married with children of their own, but to me they will always be "kid" brothers. Our fifteen-year-old nephew, Gregg, is with them. He's just completed his Hunter's Safety Course and this will be his first year at deer camp.

I help them with their gear as Robert sets the table. Soon he is ladling squirrel stew into bowls. "It's not as good as when your Dad and me make it," Robert tells them. He gives me a look and says, "I think it's those lousy red potatoes you used."

Neither Robert nor I have seen any deer, but while we're eating he tells about the big buck he jumped this morning. I find myself making suggestions on where each of us should stand at daybreak. Oddly, my recommendations have the sound of commands. I offer Gregg a spot where he's most likely to see a deer. His expression is one of disdain.

"I don't have to stand there, do I?" Gregg asks. "I can go where I want, can't I?"

"You'll go where you're told," Robert tells him, in a voice that discourages further objections. Robert draws me aside and with a wink he whispers, "You've got to let them know right off who's the boss."

The next morning—as always—Robert is the first to take a buck. He watched the forkhorn pass within a hundred yards of Gregg's stand, and then halt when the boy began to stamp his icy feet. Gregg never saw the deer slink away through the popples, and the deer never saw Robert sitting on his favorite cedar stump. One shot from Robert's ancient .30/40 Krag dropped the buck.

Gregg is crushed. Because he tried to warm his feet, he has missed the chance for a shot.

"You've got to be quiet on a stand," Robert tells him. "You were making more noise than a pack of wolves."

Things get no better as the season progresses. By midweek the deer have grown wary and are no longer moving so freely. My brothers talk Gregg into driving an alder swamp. "The deer are in the thick stuff," they tell him. So Gregg claws his way through the tangles and kicks up a six-pointer; but in the alders, there's not even room for Gregg to raise his gun. The deer moves ahead to where Mike and Steve are waiting. By the time Gregg stumbles out of the thicket, my brothers are dragging the deer back to camp.

Gregg is silent, but his frustration is evident. This business of hunting deer is not as easy as he thought. Worse yet, Robert has taken to calling him "Puppy," and as the newest member of our group, Gregg becomes the object of every joke. He endures the good-natured insults and incessant demands to fetch wood, wash dishes, and wait on us like a maid. Deer camp must mean a lot to Gregg for him to put up with the hazing, but I think he knows that one day it will be his turn to hurl the jokes.

By the end of the week, Gregg's tag is still pinned to his coat. Robert teases him about it, but when we're alone, the old man admits that he'd like to see Gregg get a shot. Robert suggests a tactic that always produces deer, though it requires more stamina than either of us really can muster. In the end, we agree to do it, because in Gregg we see something of ourselves.

* * *

Early the next morning, we set Gregg down on a ridge top overlooking a tamarack swamp. Steve gives him the scoped .270. The swamp is speckled with tiny, hemlock-clad islands—foot-high mounds of moist duff, no bigger than backyards. People seldom go there and deer seem to know it. When hunted hard, deer move to the islands and stay bedded beneath the hemlocks. It's impossible for a man to penetrate the tamaracks without making noise; when that happens, the deer slip off the islands to stand in knee-deep water, or move to the ridge until the danger has passed. Our plan is to drive the deer from the islands. Perched where he is, Gregg should see them and have a clear shot.

As soon as we enter the swamp, three deer bolt from the nearest island. Mike—the only one among us with a scope—announces they are does. It's rough going in the tamarack tangles; the spongy muskeg trembles with every step. More than once we plunge through the heather, trip over tussocks, and nick our shins on stubs. Robert complains that he's getting too old for this.

I look up at the ridge where Gregg is sitting. Once, long ago, I sat on that ridge while my father and Robert pushed this same swamp. That was the day I shot my first buck. At the time, I was only aware of having killed a deer; I knew nothing of what my father and Robert had given me. Only now, years later, do I appreciate their gift, or understand that the legacy is mine for safekeeping. Already it is passing to another.

Halfway through the swamp, a small herd of deer leaves the cover of an island. Single-file, they move through the stunted tamaracks toward the ridge. They are too far away for us to tell buck from doe. As the last of them steps into the hillside birches, Gregg begins to shoot.

"I hope one of them had horns," Robert says.

Long before we reach the birches, we can hear Gregg shouting. He is there, at the bottom of the ridge, hopping around like a toad on a griddle. Nearby, a yearling spike lies in the snow.

"I got him!" Gregg shouts. "I got him! I got him!" Then he looks at us like the boy that he is and asks, "What do I do now?"

"You can open your eyes," Robert tells him. He winks at Gregg and mutters something about a lucky shot.

We offer our congratulations and help Gregg with his deer. Soon we have the buck in tow. Something has changed for Gregg, and he knows it. Now he is one of us; now he belongs.

Even though they are dragging the animal, Gregg and my brothers quickly outdistanced Robert and me. At the end of the swamp I fall back with Robert as he stops to catch his breath. He takes a long, last look at the tamaracks, like a man who says goodbye and knows he won't return.

For Robert and my father, something is ending; but for Gregg it is just about to begin. Today, Gregg is aware only that he has shot a deer. He is too young to appreciate what he's been given, or to know that one day the legacy must be relayed. We hear him laughing as he moves toward the cabin, and toward the day when he, too, becomes keeper of the flame.

ELEVEN

Bogtrotter

A "bogtrotter" is a person who lives in or frequents bogs. I guess that describes me and most snipe hunters.

My affection for the common snipe began in high school. Back then, Rome Pond was a vast, flooded swale where the water was ankle-deep, the rushes stood knee-high, and hummocks lay scattered like islands. Its muddy meadows and water-skimmed bogs were typical snipe cover, and in early autumn the birds burst like firecrackers from every tuft of grass. Occasionally, I'd even bag one.

Nowadays, I live beside Lake Superior, surrounded by water and spruce-rimmed moors. To be sure, much has changed over the years, but my fondness for snipe hasn't. I'm a bogtrotter.

I can't think of another game bird I associate with the word "flabbergast." Ruffed grouse are explosive, black ducks are wary, sharptails are a challenge, and pheasants are smart. But snipe are just plain *dazzling*. I've probably flushed a thousand snipe, yet the next one I jump will leave me as breathless and astonished as the first.

Maybe it's the way snipe catapult into the air from under your feet: before you know the bird is there, it's gone. Quicker and more unpredictable than woodcock, jacksnipe seem as swift as bluebills. A common mistake is to shoot behind them and then not risk a second shot because the birds look out of range—an illusion due to their small size. Friends of mine who are deadly on teal are quickly humbled by jacksnipe.

In all my life, I've known only a handful of bogtrotters. Perhaps it's because most people today think of snipe as "bonus" birds: it's fine if you bag one, and it's fine if you don't. Yet nothing can match the pleasure and satisfaction of taking a brace of jacksnipe. Federal regulations allow a daily limit of eight birds, but if I drop three snipe with five shells I get to feeling smug.

Snipe are often shot by hunters jump-shooting ducks; the inexperienced among them will believe they've bagged a woodcock. But snipe are more pale and sleek, have longer legs and wings, a smaller breast, and a white belly. When flushed, a woodcock's wings make a trilling sound, but snipe cry out with a squeak.

Jacksnipe are the first migratory game bird to appear in many places. Flocks arrive and settle into marshes and sloughs from early September until freeze-up, lingering for a day or a month before vanishing overnight. Like woodcock, snipe use their long bill to probe the soil for food, but a snipe's bill can only probe wet earth. In fact, I've never seen a snipe that wasn't standing in or at the edge of water.

I'd like to have seen the teeming flocks of the 1880s that allowed sharpshooters like Captain Bogardus to bag 150 snipe in one day. In Louisiana, J. J. Pringle killed 78,000 snipe in ten years. Today, the only way to consistently find and shoot snipe is to slog through waterlogged swales until your hip boots drag like cement weights. It's hard, strenuous work, fraught with inguinal strains and chest pains; but you always have the bogs to yourself, and that sense of paludal solitude is as much a part of the hunt as are the birds.

* * *

To be sure, snipe are as delectable as partridge, but their breast is only a little larger than a chestnut. This may explain why snipe are unjustly snubbed by those who mistake "bigger" for "better."

Some years ago I took an insurance executive snipe hunting, and the two of us bagged six birds in ten hours. Back at the cabin, I braised the birds in sunflower oil, added salt, pepper, sour cream, and Bordeaux, and served them with hot cornbread and a salad. The V.P. stared at the snipe, disdainfully.

"Six little, lousy birds," he said. "Together, they're not enough to make a sandwich."

Obviously, he wasn't a bogtrotter.

Only a bogtrotter appreciates the enchantment of hunting a morass or mire where others never dare to tread. When the swale grass turns tawny and green hillsides stand flecked with gold, every flooded fen looks as promising as a rainbow.

Then, too, I like light, quick-handling, 20-gauge guns. I like open chokes, twin loads of No. 8's, and the heft of lead shot. I like hunting in shirtsleeves and an old, canvas vest, and hip boots that make me feel as though I can go anywhere. I like the way snipe flush into the breeze as they zigzag, twist, and dart; and how, after ten yards (and tremendous patience on my part), they provide a broadside target as their flight levels out.

I like that snipe do not sit as tight as woodcock, and that dogs are not needed to flush or retrieve them. And I like the snipe's predilection for giving shooters second chances: when flushed but not shot at, snipe fly in a low, wide loop, often returning to streak past me. At other times, they'll complete their loop and land nearby to be jumped again. When flushed from the windward, snipe zigzag at the hunter in a frantic rush; but if you let the birds fly past, you'll get a straightaway shot.

Most of all, I like the lush solitudes of moors, the unbroken silences of fens, and the way a bog's sense of abundant isolation makes me feel like a rich man. All of which makes me agree with Thoreau: "That man is the richest whose pleasures are the cheapest."

Some men, if they're lucky, eventually find the bird for which they're perfectly suited. For some it's grouse, and for others it's pheasants or doves. But for me, it will always be the common snipe.

I'm a bogtrotter.

TWELVE

Stolen Hours

It's three o'clock in the afternoon and I'm free for the rest of the day. It's also the first Wednesday in November and probably the end of duck season in my neck of the woods. Every pothole in my corner of northwestern Wisconsin will be frozen fast by morning.

It's been a short season of not enough time and too few ducks—mallards mostly, and some woodies and ringnecks. The tide of bluebills I expected never arrived—but it might. And that's reason enough to pay a final visit to Tinker Lake.

I'm always ready for these unexpected opportunities—when appointments are unexpectedly canceled, or I'm lucky enough to complete a project ahead of deadline. A salesman I used to know called them the "stolen hours."

"Stolen?" I asked him. "Stolen from who?"

"From the person I'd likely be," he said, "if I didn't fish and hunt."

He kept his outdoor gear in the trunk of his car so that when a late appointment didn't show up he could head for the nearest stream or patch of popples. As I remember, he was only an average shot yet he bagged over thirty partridges each year—and all within an hour's drive of his home.

"How do you do it?" I asked.

"I do what you do," he replied, "but I do it every chance I get."

In recent years I've adopted his habit. During trout season, I keep a pack rod with a small box of spinners and jigs in my Ford. In September, I toss in a shotgun, a box each of lead and steel shot, and a bag of decoys. My waders and an old camo coat stay stashed in the trunk from April through November. Always prepared, I'm ready to leave on a moment's notice whenever the opportunity arises, as it did today.

It takes thirty-five minutes to drive from my home to Tinker Lake. By the time I set out the decoys and get situated in my blind, it will be four o'clock. That leaves me sixty minutes before shooting hours close at 5:00 P.M. To my way of thinking, these sixty minutes are a blessing.

Of course, not everyone sees it as a godsend. My wife claims my desire for more hunting time has become an obsession. She believes that because I'm now "fifty-something," I've grown keenly aware of my own mortality and feel driven to exact as much as I can from life before old age or death takes it all away. And my son—who used to gladly skip high school to join me on these forays—now thinks I'm crazy for even suggesting he skip a college math class to sit in a flooded blind for an hour.

"There's more to life than having *fun*," he tells me, a little too severely for my tastes.

Of course there's more to life than fun. Indeed, fun takes up very little of the time we're allotted in this world. But I don't need a college kid telling me that; it's like a Presbyterian telling the Pope he needs to be more Catholic.

For me there's no hesitation. By four o'clock I'm hunkered down beside Tinker Lake, even though the sky is too blue for ducks. In the southwest, the setting sun is a fiery, red ball above the jackpines.

A flock of mergansers paddles in among my decoys. Across the lake a stand of broken rice is ignited by the last, level rays of sunlight. For a moment, the sere, brown rice is aflame in gleaming gold. Then an owl calls and darkness rushes in.

Friends who join me on these spontaneous, late-in-the-day, spur-of-the-moment, midweek excursions seldom ask to come along again. Whether it's duck hunting, steelhead season, bass fishing, or a walk through the grouse woods, they claim a mere hour or two of hunting and fishing isn't worth the effort—it's not practical, they insist. But they miss the point.

I used to feel it wasn't worth the effort to hunt sharptails when the birds were common in Wisconsin, and I was younger and a much better shot. I seldom hunted sharptails because the bag limit was just a token bird or two, whereas the law allowed me to take five times as many ducks or ruffed grouse. Besides, I was sure the sharptails would always be there for me, and they were—until time destroyed Wisconsin's prairies. Some years ago, when I shot my last Wisconsin sharptail, 12,400 birds were taken in the state that fall. Last year, only 45 were taken. As much as I hate to admit it, I may never again have the chance to hunt sharptails in my home country.

Now, sitting beside Tinker Lake, I look down at an old gun that is as familiar to me as my own reflection. We've been together longer than I can recall. How many ducks have I shot in that time? Surely more than I will bag in days to come. In the silence, I can clearly hear my watch ticking.

Suddenly and without warning, a flock of bluebills appears. They come hurtling out of the sky as unexpectedly as a comet. I hear them before I see them—the rush of air through their wings mimicking the sound of shredding canvas. In an instant so swift I can't even react, the bluebills realize the decoys are fake, turn away, and climb. I'm probably close enough to shoot, but by the time I'm sure of it the ducks are amoeba-like specks against the sky. Besides, it's almost 5:00 P.M.

This sort of thing used to frustrate me, back when I still hunted sharptails. But lately life has changed and now I'm happy just to be here, because it's the being here that matters. It's the only thing that does.

The temperature is falling. My fingers curl up and grow numb as I haul in the last decoys. Winter is coming—soon every lake will be sealed in ice. Overhead, bluebills speed through the dusk toward an end that cannot be known; a part of me flies away with them as they disappear into the dark. I look up to thank my lucky star, aware that every star is providential, their ancient light a silent benediction for those of us who keep these stolen hours.

THIRTEEN

Wild Goose Chase

I am always listening for the sound of geese whenever the gray winds of November begin to blow. It has to do with some unfinished business that began in boyhood, long ago. That was the autumn I tired of squirrels and rabbits, and decided to set my sights on bigger game. That was the season when I decided that, more than anything else, I needed to bag a Canada goose.

Although bringing down a goose was the next best thing to bagging a buck in the camps where I first learned to hunt, my dream of taking a goose had nothing to do with earning the respect of my older mentors. Instead, I took to hunting geese because of the way I felt whenever I heard them calling in the distance. The sound and sight of a flock battling headwinds in a cold, November sky never failed to fill me with strange and restless feelings. Their sorrowful cries were like a call from another world—a gray and ghostly world that I could only dream about. I wanted to share their sense of wild freedom, and follow the lure of those long and lonely distances into which they disappeared. To a young boy looking for adventure, the cry of wild geese was the call of wilderness.

All that autumn I would lie awake in bed at night, dreaming and scheming on how to take my first goose. I knew you could never tell when a flock might appear, and so I never left the hunting shack without a pair of goose loads in my pocket. Almost all my memories of that autumn have something to do with Canada geese: Even when I wasn't hunting, the geese were always there. I would see them on my way to school, those long skeins of undulating flecks floating like banners on the wind. I would hear them at night as they passed through the dark, their cries addling my sleep with a hunter's dreams of tomorrow. Always, the geese were there.

Because of that, I was sure I would have no trouble in bagging a goose; then came that first day along the Fox River.

I had taken the skiff and gun out alone, intending to do some pass shooting for canvasbacks. But I had hardly positioned the skiff among the rushes, when suddenly the wind changed, snow began to blow, and the sky came to life with the calling of geese.

Flocks of the big birds came down the long sweep of the river, their honking rising and falling with the wind. They were low enough that I could clearly see their white chinstraps, and although I was plainly visible in the open boat, the big gray geese never once veered away.

A full box of goose loads was stashed in the skiff, and the boat was soon littered with spent hulls. Yet all I had to show for it was a bruised and sore shoulder; not even a feather fell down from the gunmetal-gray clouds.

At the hunting shack that evening I was the butt of all the old-timers' jokes, but for once their jeers never touched me. For the sound of those geese lingered in my mind like a siren's song, filling me with a joy and sense of wonder that only another goose hunter could know.

* * *

The calling of geese was often the only thing I brought back from my days afield that autumn. Many times I sloshed through miles of mire and muck, only to sit in a flooded blind while teeming flocks of geese passed high out of range in a blueberry sky. Sometimes, when I returned to camp at the end of such days, my young friends would be waiting, gloating over a brace of woodcock or partridge they had taken, and again I would be the object of everyone's jokes. But it didn't matter. Somehow, it was enough to have spent time in a place where the geese had been flying and where I had heard them calling, watching them weave their way through space toward some point I could not perceive.

I didn't know—and couldn't explain—why simply going through the motions of hunting geese was just as good as getting a shot. Part of it was the thrill of hearing them call long before they came into view, and the delicious sense of anticipation while quietly waiting for them to wing their way into range. But there was also the feeling that something more than getting a shot was at a stake, something even more important than the geese themselves. It had to do with hopes and dreams, and with a young boy's belief that nothing was impossible.

Then one afternoon, late in the season, I finally had the perfect chance to take my goose. I was following a trail through a frozen bog, toward a patch of wild rice where bluebills lingered until ice-up. But when I reached the end of the tamaracks I saw that the rice was empty—ice was already forming among the stiff, brown stalks. I knew my dream of bagging a goose was over. Soon the lakes would be frozen fast and the last flocks of waterfowl would be far to the south.

Then I heard it—only a vague hint of that plaintive call, but enough to stop me, transfixed, at the edge of the trees. The flock was nowhere in sight and instantly the honking vanished; but then it was back, closer than before, and instinctively I snapped open the gun. I pocketed the duck loads and filled the double with twin loads of BBs.

I spotted the wedge as the geese came in over the far end of the swamp, the naked tamaracks trembling with the sound of the calls. I stayed as motionless as an oak among the larches, knowing the geese would need to pass directly in front of me to drop into the rice. They circled once, high overhead, scouting for danger. Then they began their slow descent.

I turned from the waist for a better shot through the trees; as I did, the bog burst into bedlam. The geese seemed to halt in midair, within a stone's throw of where I stood, as the swamp quickly filled with the sounds of confusion. Aware of my presence, the geese cried in alarm. I watched their broad wings beat madly at space as the flock fought frantically to climb back up into the sky.

Even then there was time for a shot. I could have emptied both barrels and reloaded if needed. But the geese and their magic were at work, and I stood dumbstruck. I watched as the geese rose and climbed out of range. When I finally looked down at my old, familiar Stevens, it was as if I were seeing that gun for the first time.

That night the temperature plunged into the low, single digits, and in the morning every lake and pond was sealed shut with ice. Soon after that the season closed, and it was spring before I heard the call of wild geese again.

I nearly died of a broken heart, and sometimes I think a small part of me did. I doubted if any boy ever wanted a wild goose as much as I did that autumn, yet it seemed the entire season had been nothing but a waste of time for me. For long afterward I believed the things you wanted most in life were always out of range. It got to the point where I swore I would never risk a broken heart again. But now—much older, and hopefully a little wiser—I realize it wasn't the geese I was hunting so much as it was the dream.

I've had other dreams since then—lofty dreams of hunting and life—and though the quarry has all too often escaped me, I'd rather risk another wild goose chase tomorrow than never dare to pursue a dream at all. And maybe that's why simply being in a blind when geese are calling is just as good as getting a shot, for in failing to bag a goose I learned a hunter's hardest lesson: the chase is transilient; dreams are not.

FOURTEEN

Just One More

In my small corner of the world, grouse season ends on New Year's Eve, but most bird hunters hang up their guns long before Thanksgiving. By then, deep snow has closed the logging trails and thickets, and travel is a matter of snowshoes and skis. Besides, everyone knows the best hunting takes place in October, before the year's young birds have been shot at and dispersed. Yet the last days of the season may bring the most memorable shooting. Certainly, they help make a long winter a bit easier to endure.

In the North, winter may arrive any time in November, when hunting shacks are vacant and shuttered and no one is abroad in the land to disrupt its feel of solitude and loneliness. The frozen earth lies rigid, every lake is locked in ice, and the bare branches of aspens weave a stark tracery against a colorless sky.

One morning in November, I left the cabin to find the woods gripped in a hush. In the air was a breathless expectation, a sense of waiting and watching as the gray sky filled with clouds. Gone now were the small, dry rustlings of autumn, the chatter of red squirrels, and the calls of chickadees. The quiet lay like a crushing weight on everything, a prelude to the silences that winter would bring.

I wanted to try for one more bird before the storm broke and winter changed the pace of life. I headed for a tamarack swamp along a chain of tiny lakes; at the edge of the muskeg where the land began to rise, ruffed grouse would be lying in the laurel and dogwood. Dry leaves crackled like cellophane as I walked downhill toward the swamp. The grouse were anxious and alert to every sound; I could hear the birds flushing far ahead of me.

But things improved when I reached the heather. Though starched with frost, the muskeg's mat was still soft and giving, and by walking its edge I could move without a sound. Now the birds bolted from the hillside, close enough to hit with a rock. I stopped to rest after an hour, and to admire the two birds tucked in my vest.

Only then did I notice the muted rustling. Not a blade of grass quivered, not a leaf fluttered, yet everywhere was a soft, whispering sound. It was snowing, and in a moment the air was white with drifting flakes. Down they came, speckling the earth, clinging to rocks and logs and fallen leaves until the brown earth was no longer merely mottled, but solidly cloaked in white.

The woods filled quickly with wet, heavy snow. Visibility decreased as the flakes floated down, obliterating landmarks. The quiet was complete now; the calm, profound. Autumn with its riotous color and excitement was over. Winter had returned to the North.

A month later, twenty inches of snow lay on the ground. No longer were the grasses showing, or the stiff, dry stems of asters and weeds. Windfalls and stumps were completely covered, and in open places the earth was a smooth, white expanse. Balsams and spruces were heavily laden; slender birches were bending low. It was always cold, and the sun appeared for only a little more than a half-dozen hours each day.

After breakfast one morning, I took the gun and snowshoes and broke trail along a logging road. In an aspen copse I found where ruffed grouse had been at work; their tracks were everywhere in the trees, and in a clump of rosy sumac where they had fed on seeds. Wing marks showed where the birds had plunged into snowbanks to spend the nights; I kicked open one drift and found an empty, ice-encrusted bed. With so much evidence, I was sure the birds were nearby. As the sun rose and warmed the day, they would break out of their burrows to feed on aspen buds.

The first grouse burst from a snowbank at the edge of the aspens. It took me by surprise, and all I could do was watch its wild, twisting flight through the trees. Then two more exploded like firecrackers from a drift. The first bird streaked ahead toward a ridge and was almost to the rise when I dropped it; the other flew behind me, hurtling through space for the balsams at my back. I turned from the waist and fired, amazed to see the grouse tumble into the snow.

I picked up the birds and turned toward home. Any other shooting I might find would be anticlimactic. I had made a double on grouse, the first in many seasons. It seemed a fine way to end the year.

* * *

To be sure, there are many ways to while away a long, northern winter. There are rabbits to chase, squirrels to hunt, and even time enough to take a second deer with a bow. There are walleyes to catch, sturgeon to spear, and beneath the ice of Lake Superior the trout will be hitting. Yet for all that, I am never ready to accept winter and its ruthless finality. The end of the year means more than snow, cold, and ice. It also means that time is growing shorter.

So it was that on New Year's Eve I went back into the woods. There was time to take one more bird before the season ended, and it seemed wrong not to make the most of that. It was ten above zero, and the only sound in the icy silence was the creak of my snowshoes as I shuffled over the crust of the trail where I had made the double.

On a far ridge, the setting sun was a vermillion globe of quivering fire; as it sank it drained all color from the sky. The tote road weaved its way through a stark and barren country, a land of black spruce, gray birch, and white snow. There was no stirring, no rustling, no hint of sound or movement. Life had changed in the North; its pulse was weak, and barely felt. Staying alive was the only aim of every creature, and only the strongest would survive until spring, when green ridges would tremble again with the sound of drumming grouse.

On both sides of the trail, white birches stood like picked bones. A gust of wind rattled the trees, accentuating the silence. The sun was setting quickly and darkness was rushing in. I stepped up on the crest of a drift, and when I did a big partridge burst like a bomb from the snow.

It sent me reeling, and I would have lost sight of the bird had it flow any distance; but it only sailed into the top of a birch, and began to bud, unconcerned. It was an easy shot and no one was looking, but it would have been a terrible way to end the year.

The bird tottered precariously on the high, lithe branches, losing its balance at times but keeping itself aloft with frantic wing beats. As I watched, a last, level ray of sunlight struck the birch tops. When it did, the purple branches all but flamed. The trunks of the trees glistened like silver rapiers; even the grouse appeared dazzling in the light—the dull, brown bird now gleamed like amber. In a world where all the elements were intent on crushing survival, the grouse was a testament to life's quiet perseverance.

The image lasted only an instant. The sun fell away and darkness flooded in. The grouse lost its luster and flew away into the timber. I never raised my gun.

I had gone out with the hope of bagging a bird; instead, I saw a phoenix rise from a snowy tomb. The year was done and grouse season was over. Now I was ready for winter, and whatever it might bring.

FIFTEEN

Root River

Yesterday I paid a visit to the past and tarried beside the Root River. As a boy, the Root was the end of my backyard: it was as far as my friends and I could wander in a day and still return home before dark.

I was surprised at how little the river had changed. The stone bridge where we used to catch bluegills was exactly as I remembered. The Root's banks were still clad in huge willows; beyond them, pheasants cackled in the corn as they always had. Downstream, a big beech still bore the wound of my first love, its smooth, blue bark scarred with a heart I'd carved long ago with a Barlow knife—inside the heart were Claire's and my initials.

The Root winds its way through the cornfields, canary grass, and suburbs of southeastern Wisconsin; as a boy, its every bend was as familiar to me as my name. Here, as youngsters, my friends and I caught crayfish, stalked turtles, and hunted grizzlies with cattail spears. In summer we'd wade into the mud to pan for gold with my mother's pie tins, or we'd borrow someone's garden spade to dig for buried treasure along the banks. And at least once a year, a bunch of us would build a raft from old crates and baling wire, and float downstream in search of the Northwest Passage.

I don't know if kids still do these sorts of things. Not long ago, when I told my neighbor's twelve-year-old about the things I did as a boy, he asked if I had grown up poor. Only now, looking back, do I realize how lucky I was to have grown up along the Root River.

* * *

As teenagers, Rick and I would walk to the Root in the early dark of weekend mornings, while pheasants cackled in the marsh grass on either side of the road. We'd jump-shoot the river for ducks, usually taking a couple of woodies, and then hunt the pheasants as we headed back home through the fields.

Around noon we'd stop in an abandoned orchard to dine on apples. We'd take the birds from our vests, carefully lay them in the tawny grass beneath the trees, and admire each bird's size and color while recounting every detail of the morning's hunt.

After lunch, we'd lie back against the shaggy bark of a hickory and look out across a golden landscape under a blue sky flecked with white clouds. High overhead, skeins of Canada geese rippled like pennants in the wind, steadily moving toward a place as distant and unknown to us as tomorrow.

"Do you think things will always be this great?" I once asked.

"No," Rick said. "They'll be better."

Nothing is as wonderful as a boy. He can go anywhere and do anything, and never leave his backyard. To a boy, nothing is impossible and life is an infinite series of tomorrows. And though life changes, the boy in us need never grow old.

If we're lucky, that everlasting boy lives on as our secret self—that private part of us we try to hide from others, but that wives and mothers sometimes see. The lad who lives in me still gets as wildly excited as if it were Christmas each time I pack for deer camp; and though he's no longer quite as quick when it comes to shooting grouse, he's still unbeatable when it comes to day-dreams.

The boy in me climbs deer stands and sets out decoys in the darksome, early hours of autumn mornings, and probably spends too much time in johnboats and canoes. He's as hopeful on the last day of duck season as he was on the first, and on a trout stream he genuinely believes the fish of a lifetime lies in the next pool. And when I'm wet, cold, skunked, and more than just a bit lost, he's there to remind me that any day spent outdoors is a good day, and one worth living.

* * *

The Root River has weathered the years much better than I have. Its willow-clad banks remain unchanged, and its pheasants still cackle—though not as loudly. To be sure, the children with whom I shared that stream have vanished, except for the small boy who keeps me company wherever I roam. As kids go, he's not too demanding: all he asks is to always have a stretch of trout water to fish, and maybe a patch of woodcock cover to explore. And, of course, some extra tomorrows—extra tomorrows, galore.

SIXTEEN

Burning Bright

There's an old tree stand in the woods where I usually hunt. Whenever I pass it, I feel compelled to stop. The rough-sawn boards of its frame are as gray as an old gun barrel. The rotted planks that form its deck are as loose as bad teeth.

I have no idea who built the stand. It was already long abandoned and useless when I found it in this remote corner of Wisconsin, twenty years ago. Since then, the white pine that supports it has succumbed to blister rust. The tree is tottering and dead—it will not last the winter—and when it falls, it will take with it my only link to a life lived long ago and now forgotten.

Although I don't know who built the stand, I do know something about the man. It's obvious the fellow knew his stuff. He built his stand at the top of a ravine, eight feet off the ground. An isolated patch of oaks—rare in this boreal forest—grows on both sides of the chasm, and even now the long grass under those trees is crosshatched with the trails of deer seeking acorns. At the bottom of the chasm is a spring—I have seen deer drink at the pool from August to freeze-up. West of the stand is an old field that was once seeded with alfalfa; at its edge lie encroaching aspens. Over the years, I have taken deer early in the morning at the edge of the field and late in the day among the oaks near the spring—all of which were dropped within 100 yards of the old stand.

A wooden ladder used to lean against the stand. Pieces of it now lie in the duff's dry needles. A rusty coil of barbed wire hangs from a stub below the stand. Nearby, in the field, is an old brown hayrake, the sort that was hitched to horses.

No one has farmed this land for over fifty years, yet the barbed wire and the hayrake are haunting—as though the farmer who left them here intends to return at any moment. I listen for the sound of footsteps, the lowing of cattle, or the distant calls of children. There is only the sound of the dead pine and its forgotten stand, creaking in the wind.

People tell me there was a farm on this spot until the 1940s, the last one in the township. By then, the pioneers who settled here just before the 1920s had given up on farms that yielded only stumps, rocks, and heartache. Loggers used the abandoned fields to keep horses until skidders and gasoline became cheaper than making hay. When I first hunted here in the 1970s, all the land within a week's walk had been logged over, every sawmill was gone, and only ten people lived in the entire township. Now, twenty years later, no one lives here at all. In less that eighty years—the length of a lifetime—the land has gone from wilderness to a logging community, and back to wilderness again.

So much for the constancy of men.

* * *

On this November afternoon, a week before Thanksgiving, I'm sitting on a log below the stand, cleaning a pair of partridge in the almost-frozen spring at the bottom of the chasm. The two birds will likely be the last I take this season, and the memory of this day will have to last an entire year until I hunt birds again next autumn.

I slip the birds into my game vest and walk uphill toward the abandoned stand, wondering what memories it gave to the man who built it. I imagine him on that stand on an icy November morning, clad in his wool mackinaw and Malone pants, cursing at the cold and snow, the price of deer tags and cartridges, and the whitetail that was there and gone before he knew it.

I wonder how many sandwiches he ate while perched on that stand? How many cigarettes did he smoke; how many times did he forget his matches? It's easy for me to imagine him stamping his feet, trying to pump blood through toes as numb as ice. How often did he force himself to stay put rather than move?

I wonder if the man had children. If so, did those youngsters take their first deer from this stand? It's a secret I will never unravel. Only the ravine's old oaks remember if these woods rang with shouts of joy and laughter.

Most of all, I wonder what became of the people who hunted from this stand. The youngest of them would be silver-haired by now, as gray as the weathered pine boards on which they spent the happiest hours of their youth. Do they still hunt, or ever think of this place? The silence of this haunted land is my answer.

Like the crumbling colonnades of a lost world, the abandoned tree stand makes me painfully aware of life's swift impermanence. Deer still bed in the alfalfa and drink at the chasm's spring, but the man who built this stand is a ghost. I, who felt a kinship with the past, suddenly feel the terrible press of time. I, who spent a leisurely afternoon hunting birds, have become the one pursued.

In the gathering dusk an owl calls. I quicken my pace to be out of the woods before dark. But on a distant ridge, the setting sun totters like a trembling red globe, igniting the sky with the blazing fire of its afterglow. I stop to savor the moment, thrilled by the fiery sunset, and no longer anxious about cheating time. To be sure, more than daylight burns as I watch. But while it lasts, the light it casts is lovely.

PART THREE

TAIL FEATHERS AND BACKLASH

SEVENTEEN

Fishing with Bubba

One of the few things I've asked of life is to be blessed with a good companion, a gentle man with a sensitive soul for whom hunting and fishing are a kind of spiritual communion. He'd be able to recite William Cullen Bryant's "To a Waterfowl" while killing time in a duck blind, or hum a bit of Bach when casting to a rise. He'd be a quintessential woodsman of Thomistic tastes and cultured desires who could find magic in a sunset, the call of geese, or a campfire.

Instead, life has given me a companion who answers to the name of "Bubba." To Bubba, Bach is a brewer of inferior beer.

"Bach? Yeah, I've had *bock* beer," Bubba once said. "It's dark and it's brown and tastes lousy!"

As for woodmanship, no one comes close to Bubba—especially when he's building a fire.

"I'd take it easy with that gasoline," I told him.

"Quit meddling!" he snapped. "I'm the cook and I'll build the fire my way."

It's been a year now, and I'm beginning to wonder if Bubba's eyebrows will ever come back.

Through some cruel trick of chance, we happen to be related: Bubba is my kid brother, younger by more years than I care to recall. We belong to different generations, which may explain our differences. I, for instance, belong to a time when English was the common language of American sportsmen.

An example of what I mean occurred last September when Bubba stopped in to make plans for the Labor Day weekend.

"Figgered we'd take my hawg-findin' rig and hit those honey holes on Clam Lake," he said. "I was out there last weekend, a-throwin' in some bodacious-lookin' cabbage, when I got a bump from this humongous bucketmouth that was bigger than my bait's bin."

I stared at him—the pride of Wisconsin's finest university—and marveled at what a college education can do for a young man nowadays. "Oh," I finally said, not sure what to make of it. "I thought we were going fishing."

Bubba gave me a patient look. "You know," he said, "there is more to life than brook trout."

"You're right," I told him. "There's *brown* trout—the kind that should be hitting on the upper Namekagon. I thought we'd head over there and work the Squaw Bend area. Of course, to fish it properly, we'll have to float that stretch with a canoe."

"I dunno," Bubba said. "I never fished from a boat that wasn't equipped with swivel seats."

"Ah," I said, "then you're going to discover what *real* fishing is all about—how an angler has to work at tricking a fish before he can truly enjoy his catch."

"Work?" Bubba asked. He shook his head. "There you go again, meddling in my affairs. If I wanted to work, I'd get a job."

* * *

The Namekagon begins in northwestern Wisconsin near the town of Cable. In the old days the Namekagon was a major route of the fur trade, and on maps used by early French explorers it was referred to as the East Fork of the St. Croix. Along with the St. Croix, the Namekagon was one of the original streams designated as a wild river by the National Wild and Scenic Rivers Act of 1968. Since then, the Namekagon is no longer the secret it once was, but in September, after summer's crowds have left the North, the river is as alone as it used to be.

We made arrangements in town for a pickup and shuttle, and then parked where the river crosses U.S. 63. This stretch of stream downstream to Seely—some six or seven miles distant—is one of the wilder sections of the upper Namekagon. Famous for its smallmouths, northerns, walleyes, and even an occasional muskie, here, near its headwaters, the Namekagon is home to big browns.

Only after we had reached the river did I first suspect Bubba's fear of canoes. It started with his screams.

"Watch out for that log! Get away from those rocks! Look out! Look out! We're tipping! We're tipping!"

"Good Lord, Bubba. Settle down, will you?" We were still at the landing, trying to lift the canoe off the roof of our car.

His dread of canoes was easier to understand once we were on the water. The river was high and swift, and the rushing urgency of the current quickly swept us downstream—backward. From the first stroke, Bubba did everything in his power to swamp us. Seated in the bow, he dug at the water in quick, choppy strokes like a murderer feverishly digging a grave for his victim. He had no coordination, and his paddle switched from side to side like a metronome ticking time to a polka.

"Take it easy," I told him. "All we want to do is keep the bow pointed straight ahead. You don't have to pull your guts out to get us to Seely."

"If you don't like the way I row, do it yourself!" He put away his paddle and took out his rod.

Things went well after that until we hit the first rapids. They weren't more than riffles, really, but when Bubba reached for his paddle I prepared for the worst.

"Easy now," I told him. "This is kid's stuff. Just watch out for—"

Thump!

"Rocks! Rocks!" Bubba shrieked.

"Push us off," I said, trying to remain calm as the tail end of our canoe began swinging sideways to the current. In an instant, water was rushing over the gunwale.

"Lean downstream!" I yelled. "Lean away from the current."

"Stop giving me orders and get us off this rock!"

Later, after we had salvaged the canoe, built a fire, and dried ourselves out, I decided the pool below those rapids was as fine a place as any to fish. Dawn and dusk, when the stream is shrouded in shadows, are the best times to try for the Namekagon's big browns, but even at high noon the chances of luring a 1-pounder out from behind a rock are often good.

On my third cast, a nice brown struck from behind a boulder. I caught a glint of color as it streaked through the icy-bright water, and later, when I had the fish in hand, he gleamed like a shiny, new penny. At fifteen inches, he wasn't one of the Namekagon's trophy trout; I released it and grinned at Bubba. Ten minutes later I caught a smallmouth that went on the stringer.

"Took them both on a Muddler," I called to Bubba. He was fishing below me and hadn't had a strike.

"When I want your two-bit advice I'll ask for it," he said. "Tell you what: I'll bet a case of Bach's beer or whatever it is you drink that I'll catch the biggest fish today."

It was a wager I couldn't pass up.

After that the serious fishing began. I picked up another bass before we hit Pacwawong Lake. At a pound it was a lovely fish, but nowhere near in size to the 3-pounders the Namekagon sometimes gives up. Bubba, sullen and silent, was obviously envious: By the time we made Pacwawong, he was still fishless.

Certainly the fishing is as good a reason as any to float the Namekagon, but the real lure of the stream is something that will never be taken home in a creel. Although 300 years have passed since Jesuit explorers first explored the river in birchbark canoes, something of the old wilderness remains. Despite bridges and farms and an occasional cabin, an old magic lingers on the water. It is there in the high banks clad in spruce and fir, and in the rip and tumble of a wild river. It is there in dark pools rimmed by ancient rocks and brooding cedars.

Most of all, it is there in the expansive sloughs of Pacwawong. It was here where nineteenth-century loggers built a dam in an effort to raise water levels to float out the country's virgin timber. The dam is a waterfall of rubble now—a dangerous spillway that must be either portaged or run by fools in canoes—but the slough it created remains, a great and abandoned swamp where the wild is always calling, but seldom heard.

We drifted across the placid waters of Pacwawong, jumping big flocks of black ducks and mallards in the maze of the slough. Shorebirds called from the mud flats and rushes, while herons bolted at the channel's every turn. Big flights of teal filled the sky, already gathering for the long journey south. Deer glided along banks that gleamed silver with weathered beaver slash, and bald eagles swooped low to pluck fish from the stream. It was an image from a once vast and teeming wilderness, a part of the past still alive and well on the Pacwawong sloughs.

I was so caught up in watching the display that I didn't notice the quickening current.

"Hey, listen to that wind," Bubba said. "It sounds like a freight train moving through the woods."

I glanced at the timbered banks: Not a leaf quivered. Bubba turned to say something just as we came around a bend where the river suddenly rushed forward without warning. He was still looking at me, babbling over his shoulder, but beyond him I saw the frothing cauldron of the broken dam.

"Right!" I screamed. "Get over to the *right*!" The portage sign was as clear as the confusion on Bubba's face.

"I can't hear you over all this wind!" Bubba called, oblivious to the danger. "Boy, we're really moving now!"

We lost the chance to portage and I dropped to my knees, aiming for a chute no wider than the canoe. Beyond the falls was a wall of standing water as high as a hearse.

"What'cha doin' on your knees?" Bubba asked. "Praying I don't catch a bigger fish than you?" He laughed. Then he turned around, and I could tell by the way his hair sprang erect that he had at last seen the falls.

Later, when the undertow spit us out several miles downstream, I swore I would never again drink, smoke, curse, miss Sunday Mass, or share a canoe with Bubba. I lay on the bank, clutching my rod and paddle in one hand and trying to keep Bubba's head underwater with the other.

When he finally struggled free, we went off to look for the canoe and our gear. Two hours later we were back on the stream, minus Bubba's flyrod. By the time we made Seely it was almost dark.

"Where's the guy who's supposed to pick us up?" Bubba asked when we made the landing.

"He probably died of old age." It had taken the two of us twelve hours to make a three-hour trip.

"Now what do we do?" Bubba asked.

In the gathering dark, the *plop* of a Namekagon brown answered the question. It was the witching hour, that time at dusk when the world stands still and seems to hold its breath. Insects were humming, a whippoorwill was calling, and on the calm, moonlit surface of the river the big browns were beginning to rise.

"Geez, ain't them bugs ever gonna stop buzzin'?" Bubba asked. "And listen to that goofy bird—he's drivin' me nuts already. Twelve stinkin' hours on this river and not one bite, and then I lose my best rod in that last spill we took." He shook his head. "I gotta tell you, this is *not* my idea of fishing."

I looked at the wretch: He was wet, cold, cut, scraped, depressed, dejected, demoralized, and, worst of all, fishless. Aw, what the heck, I thought, as I offered him my rod. Besides, I had already taken three nice fish. Who could want for anything more?

"I guess it's the least you can do," Bubba said as he grabbed my gear. "After all, if you knew how to handle a canoe, I wouldn't have lost my rod back in that whirlpool."

I ignored the remark. Instead, I suggested he make a cast downstream at the undercut bank.

"You just love giving orders, don't you?" Bubba asked. In defiance, he made a cast upstream at a pool of moonlight. "Hey! I got one!"

I could tell by the way my rod arched that Bubba had tied into one of the Namekagon's true trout. The fish kicked like a mule, and when it jumped the spray was a shower of sparks. The fish rushed him, and Bubba quickly stripped line, the coils lying like a welt on the silvery stream. He eventually brought the fish into the shallows, where I waded out and netted it.

"He's a beauty, ain't he?" Bubba asked.

It was a beautiful brown, all right: thick, fat, and all of three pounds. "I want my rod back," I said.

"Yeah, sure. Here it is. Just let me see my fish. Wow! Is he as big as he looks?"

I handed him the fish. "Don't gloat," I warned him.

"Gee," Bubba said. "My fish makes the ones you caught look like wimps. Aren't you embarrassed to keep them little bass? Anyway, you owe me a case of Bach's beer."

"This trip isn't over yet," I said.

"Sure it is," said Bubba. "Here comes the guy from the bait shop to pick us up."

I looked up at the landing and into the twin headlights of a pickup truck. Then a door slammed shut, and a familiar voice called out: "You two okay? I was about ready to have the sheriff start dragging the river. Even girl scouts don't take this long to float the Namekagon."

Bubba held his fish high in the air, making sure the beam of the headlights would strike it.

"Nice fish!" the man called. "What 'cha take him with?"

"A meddler," Bubba said.

"Don't you mean a Muddler?" the man asked.

"No, I mean a meddler," Bubba said. He nodded in my direction. "That's him over there."

There was a moment of silence, and then, even in the darkness, I could feel the sense of recognition that flooded the man's face.

"Oh, yeah," I heard him say. "I forgot. You two are brothers, ain't 'cha?"

EIGHTEEN

The Bear Facts

Most people think of bear country as a place on a map, but it actually lies in a camper's cerebrum. For a bear, no other land is quite so lush as a high-strung imagination. Not only are most bears spawned in a camper's mind, but those that dwell there thrive, growing in size and ferocity with every sound in the night, until the creatures reach full size, which is roughly big enough to straddle a tent.

An isolated campground late at night is not the spot to expect a good night's rest. The fiery crash of a UFO is only a minor curiosity compared to the snap of a twig as you're drifting off to sleep. Just the thought of sleeping in a bear's backyard can make a camper quiver. The famous Finnish woodsman and my old sidekick, Toivo Sisu, knows this and puts it to good use whenever another party has beaten us to a favorite campsite.

"Hello, there!" Toivo will call in a neighborly way as he approaches the young man and his wife. "Boy, you sure have guts to be tent-camping out here in *bear country*."

"Bear country?" the young lady will ask, her eyes scanning the brush for a tuft of black fur.

"You betch'a. You'll sure see a lot of wildlife if you camp in this spot. Just last week I was staying here and bears broke into my camper. Ripped the door off its hinges and chased my poor Martha up a tree. Of course, the bears weren't half as exciting as the Sasquatch."

By the time Toivo finishes his tale, the young couple are hightailing it for the nearest theme park.

Toivo's glee in frightening away campers is surprising, especially if you've ever shared a tent with him. Before hooking up with Toivo, I'd always thought camping was no more complicated than finding a spot to pitch a tent, but I've since learned there are many ways to make and break camp.

For instance, there's *RV camping*. "RV" stands for "rescue vehicle," which is an automobile's primary function in bear country. RV camping is when we pull into a campsite late at night and sleep in the car because Toivo thinks he "hears something."

Tent camping is when we try to pitch a tent in the dark in bear country. This usually evolves into *canoe camping*, when we stash the tent under the canoe and dash back to the car because Toivo "sees something."

Survival camping is when we actually pitch the tent and lie awake inside it, all the while wondering what our chances are of surviving a bear attack. *Primitive camping* is when we decide our chances aren't good, and then drive to a motel where the TV isn't cable.

Sometimes Toivo tries to relieve the tension of camping in bear country by playing games. His favorite is Twenty Questions. When the campfire is cold and the flashlights are dead, Toivo begins the game by asking: "Did you hear that?"

The object is to wake me so that I, too, can be scared senseless. If I'm asleep—or too terrified to move—Toivo's next question is: "Are you sleeping?"

"Do you see that?" I ask, when it's finally my turn to ask questions. Usually I'm pointing at the flickering shadow on the tent wall beside my head. Contrary to what Toivo claims, I am not a sissy. Everyone knows the shadow of a balsam tree can easily be mistaken for a serial killer.

Admittedly, the invention of commercial bear repellents has taken much of the excitement out of camping in bear country. However, when commercial repellents aren't available, you can still rely on makeshift remedies.

One of these is the empty coffee can into which a handful of pebbles are deposited. When shaken, the tiny stones create a nerve-wracking din. Should you be awakened by a suspicious sound, you can repel the bear by rattling the can. Unfortunately, every camper within earshot will also be rattled. Should you persist in being skittish, you may also need riot gear to repel a mob.

Another technique for routing bears is "the shout." The theory behind this is that bears are basically timid creatures, and that a good shout will send any bruin on its way. It will also send your partner through the roof of the tent if he's sleeping.

One night, while camping with Toivo, I was jolted from sleep by a bloodcurdling cry. I sprang awake, eyes wide open, confused by the sound of stampeding buffaloes coming from my heart.

"It's all right," Toivo said softly, "go back to sleep. I thought I heard a bear, but I guess I ran him off. I'll just step outside to check the fire."

Later, after my pulse had slowed to a rapid staccato, I was again awakened by the sound of Toivo chopping wood. This was followed by the clanking of beer cans, the endless shuffling of folding chairs, and the incinerator-like rumble of a blazing bonfire.

"Ain't no bears around here," I heard Toivo say, trying to convince himself. "Sure is a beautiful night. Just look at those stars. And, hey!—there's the Big Dipper. Wow!—look at it twinkle!"

Nights in bear country are longer when a coward tends the campfire.

As stimulating as an imaginary bear can be, it's the real ones that make camping exciting. The false alarms are idle amusement compared to what happens when a real bear shows up in camp.

Last summer we were fishing up in French Canada with Toivo's friend, Remi. At night, after cleaning our catch, Remi would toss his fish scraps toward the campfire. His aim was lousy.

"Won't all these fish guts attract bears?" I asked.

"No, no," Remi said, flicking the entrails of yet another walleye past the campfire and onto our tent. "And if zee bear shows up just give a good holler—hey? That's good enough to scare zee bear."

One night, after the campfire was out, the three of us were awakened by the sound of padded footfalls just outside our tent.

"Did you hear that?" Toivo whispered.

"Probably just a 'coon," I said.

"No raccoons in Canada," Remi said. "Probably is just a skunk. But Remi will take a peek so zee big American crybabies can sleep—hey?"

Remi crawled out of his blankets and opened the tent flaps. In front of us stood a bear as big as a beer truck. The animal had been snacking on our fish scrap hors' d'oeuvres. It was clear we were to be the pièce de résistance.

"Give him a good holler, Remi," I cried.

"GET ZEE HELL OUT OF HERE!" Remi screamed. He chucked my boots at the beast, grabbed the ax, and leaped through the tent flaps. It wasn't until Remi slammed the door of his float plane that I realized he was screaming at Toivo and me.

Later, when we were safely inside the plane, Remi said he had never seen anyone do the triple jump while encased in a sleeping bag. I told Remi he was pretty good at the 100 dash himself.

"Shut up," Toivo whispered, his face and hands pressed against the window. "I see something out there. I think it's a werewolf!"

NINETEEN

The Compleat Idler

I don't know if I'm as lazy as people claim. For one thing, I don't have the ambition to think about it.

As a boy, my father was always accusing me of being lazy. He would give me an order, like "mow the lawn," and dutifully I'd set out for the shed where the grass cutter was stored. But the shed also housed our fishing gear, and to this day I swear one of those cane poles was a magic wand. All I'd have to do was look at it and—*poof*!—instantly I'd find myself fishing the nearest stream, instead of at home, mowing the lawn.

"Honest, Dad, I don't know how it happens," I'd plead.

"I do," he'd say. "You're lazy!" Then he'd wave that cane pole at me and—*poof*!—instantly I'd be back in the shed. Usually I was lying across Dad's lap.

That was long ago but I'm still accused of being lazy. It's the kind of mean-spirited lie I ought to deny, but I don't have the energy to disagree.

I guess some jobs are just more meaningful than others. I can tote an eighty-pound canoe all day through a muskeg swamp to reach a lake where the smallmouths grow as big as salmon. But if my wife asks me to take out the trash, my back goes into spasm and I have to lie down and watch TV until the pain has passed.

Fortunately, I bounce back quickly; I'm usually feeling better by the time Peg takes out the trash.

I can't imagine what Izaak Walton was thinking when he wrote *The Compleat Angler.* In it, he claims an angler's life is the best of any: "'Tis full of pleasure, and void of strife."

Who was he kidding?

If you're an angler, there's *always* something that needs to be done, and never enough time to do it:

- My tackle box looks like a dumpster in a city where the trash collectors are out on strike.
- The loose line guide on my best flyrod is held in place with rubber bands.
- I think it's a big deal when my reels are spooled with line less brittle than straw.

Every winter I buy several spools of new line for my reels, but stripping the old monofilament from the reels is a boring and time-consuming chore. Usually I put off doing it until there's nothing better to do. Amazingly, there are a lot of better things to do than strip old line from fishing reels.

My leaky waders should have been properly patched years ago, but I've been so busy thinking about when to do it that I've temporarily patched them with duct tape. Once you've stayed dry for a whole season in waders patched with duct tape, it's a lot easier to spend the next season wrapped in duct tape, too.

It's not that I don't try to keep on top of things. When I come home from a hunting trip, I park the car in the driveway and immediately bring the guns into the house. Then I sit down to think about what to bring in next. Loading a car for a hunting trip is just as big a chore as unloading it—but there is a difference. I can pack for a trip in ten minutes; but unpacking is so loathsome I may not do it for a week.

My laid-back attitude extends to my hunting skills as well. Whereas my buddies have monikers like "Gander" or "Buck," everyone knows me by the nickname, "Slouch." My neighbor, Steelie, christened me that the first time we hunted deer together.

Steelie gets a deer every season. He claims he's successful because he does things like preseason scouting and sighting-in his rifle. But I know the real reason for his success is his tree stand.

Steelie's typical tree stand is an edifice that rivals the Taj Mahal. Construction begins in August, and by deer season his basic tree stand includes insulated seats, a roof, carpeting, and a sun deck. About the only thing his stand lacks is an elevator.

In contrast, I begin building my tree stand the day before deer season. My most elaborate model consists of a few rotten boards spiked together in the crotch of a tree. My stands aren't elegant, but they do look natural. They're so well camouflaged even I can't find them on opening day.

If there's one thing I'm not slack about, it's cleaning and preserving my catch. I diligently scale or filet, skin or pluck, and fastidiously wash whatever fish and game I take. Then I carefully wrap each item and tuck it into the freezer. But for some reason, labeling the packages seems like a bother. Besides, I have a good memory.

Would anyone like a venison roast, circa 2000? I recently found it while cleaning out my freezer. The meat should be properly aged by now.

I really don't know if I'm as lazy as people claim. Maybe I'll lie down and think about it . . . tomorrow.

TWENTY

Nailin' Toads

I had just settled down for the evening with a copy of Haig-Brown's *Fisherman's Fall* when the telephone rang. The call was from my neighbor, "HawgBuster" Olafson. For a moment, I feared my choice of titles was a harbinger of things to come.

"I've been out lookin'," HawgBuster said, "and I done found me the sweetest honey hole. You wanna go out in the mornin' and see if'n we can't nail a couple of toads?"

"Gee, Hawg, I don't know," I said, trying to beg off. "Driving nails into frogs isn't my idea of fun."

"Nailing frogs?" he asked, incredulous. "What the *hail* you talkin' about, boy?"

"What are *you* talking about?" I asked. "And what's with the Smoky-and-the-Bandit accent? The farthest south you've ever been is Milwaukee."

There was a long pause—it was HawgBuster's way of letting me know he was being tolerant.

"Man, I'm talkin' *hawgs*! *Pigs*! Good 'uns. Porkers."

"I thought you were on a low-cholesterol diet."

There was a long, exasperated sigh at the other end of the phone. "Listen. I'm talkin' *bass*. You wanna come along tomorrow and see if'n we can't bump into a couple?"

"Can I do a little fishing while you're bumping?" I asked. "I've got this new pole I've been meaning to try out and—"

Hawg broke in: "You've got a *what*?"

"A pole. A *fishing* pole. I was over at the mall last week and they had this rod-and-reel combo on sale—"

Hawg interrupted again: "You bought a stick from a shopping mall?"

"No, no. Not a stick. A fishing rod. It came with a reel and line, and I got the whole works for less than 20 bucks."

"Oh, geez," Hawg groaned, and then he gave me another long pause. Suddenly I felt as ridiculous as Hawg had looked the time he led me to a deer track that ended at the base of a squirrel tree.

"Listen. Meet me at the boat landing on Mudpuppy Lake tomorrow at sunrise," Hawg said. "And bring a stick with some *string* on it, instead of that ultralight thread you use."

"I have some baling twine," I said.

Hawg gave another long groan. "Oh, geez," he said. "Oh, geez."

* * *

I reached the landing before he did the next day, and I used the time to try and remember Hawg's real name. I've known the man for twenty years, but he changes his name more often than the bow of a canoe changes direction. During deer season he insists on being referred to as "Buck," and on a trout stream the only moniker he answers to is "Brookie." Now he was caught up in his enthusiasm for bass fishing; appropriately, he had dubbed himself "HawgBuster."

Eventually Hawg arrived at the boat landing in his jeep, towing something that looked like a top-secret landing craft for the Navy.

Hawg backed the thing down to the lakeshore. "Give me a hand launching this baby, will ya?" he asked.

"Launch? You mean it flies, too?"

Hawg gave me his patient look. "Very funny. This just happens to be a top-of-the-line Super Duper Phantom Magnum Model Twelve Bassfinder rig."

"Oh, I thought it might be a boat." I was being sincere, but I saw Hawg would never believe it.

"Where do you want me to sit?" I asked, after we'd gotten the thing into the water.

"You wanna use the throne up front?"

"No thanks. I took care of that before I left home."

Something happened to Hawg, and for a moment his face looked as red and swollen as the fluorescent plastic worms in his tackle box.

"Go sit up front on that swivel chair and shut up!" he ordered. "Shut up and pay attention and maybe you'll learn something about fishing today."

We spent the next few hours on the water, sharing the same boat on the same lake, but operating in entirely different worlds. While I tried my hand at casting, Hawg engaged in something he called "throw-un." While I kept wishing for a fish to take my lure, Hawg kept "lookin' to git bit" on his baits. At one point he began ranting and raving about the oscillations of his electronic depth sounder. "See that? And this?" He kept calling my attention to the face of the machine. Evidently something very important was happening there, but it was lost on me.

"A bassin' man may as well stay home without one of these things on his rig," Hawg said. "How else would a guy know how deep to fish?"

I looked over the side of the boat to where I had tossed the anchor. "The anchor rope's out about ten feet," I said.

Hawg gave me a malevolent look and patted his depth machine.

* * *

Eventually we cruised into a weedy bay. On the far side an old man was rowing an ancient duck skiff, trolling along the lakeshore with a cane pole hung over the skiff's transom. I watched the old-timer as he lazily worked the shallows and felt more than a little envious. There was something pure and simple about the sight. The old-timer and his primitive gear seemed to belong to the place in a way Hawg and his highly sophisticated gear would never manage. In all likelihood, the old-timer had impaled a night crawler on a rusty hook and tossed the works into the water. No machines, no undecipherable jargon, no concern for structure or thermoclines. If the fish were there, they would strike. And when they did it would be something natural, magical, and wondrous.

"Look at that old fool," Hawg said, bringing me out of my reverie. "He probably hasn't seen a fish all day."

"Neither have we," I reminded Hawg.

He waved away my remark. "That's going to change right now," he said. "This honey hole is going to produce. Just look at this surface cover. And check out the bottom structure under those stickups."

I looked around, but all I saw were lily pads, sunken logs, and the stubs of snags.

"That stickup there is a strike zone if I ever saw one," Hawg said. He nodded toward a dead tree poking up out of the water.

"That dead tree looks like a good place, too," I said.

Hawg ignored me. Instead, he picked up his stick and heaved a chocolate-scented plastic worm toward the snag.

"Hey!" Hawg suddenly shouted. "I got a strike!"

I looked at where he had tossed the worm. "Are you sure you didn't snag that old tree?"

"No. No. It's a toad, all right, and I'm gonna nail him!"

I shook my head. "There you go again, talking about driving nails into frogs."

"Nailin' toads ain't the same thing as torturing frogs!" Hawg shouted. "I've done bumped me into a lunker—and I mean *humongous*. I've got me a toad! A pig! A real porker!"

"Hawg," I said, trying to bring him back into the real world of leaky boats and worm slime, "this is northern Wisconsin. There might be a couple of nice bass in this lake. There might even be a few you could call *piglets*. But *hogs*? Real *porkers*?"

"I'm tellin' you I got me a toad!"

Hawg cranked furiously away at his reel, and the stick of his hawg-hauler bowed like a horseshoe. Hawg was excited, hopping around his bassfinder like a frog in a frying pan. By now, the old-timer had seen the excitement and was rowing across the bay to us.

"Yumpin' Yiminy, it's a big one, yah, you betch'a!" Hawg cried, lapsing into his native northern Wisconsin tongue.

The old man in his skiff was within talking distance of us now.

"Got her snagged, huh, young fella?" he asked.

"I got me a toad!" Hawg cried. "A big 'un. A sow belly!"

The old man looked at him as if Hawg were a riddle in quantum physics. Then his expression changed. "Sorry," the old-timer told me. "I didn't know your friend was afflicted."

"Here she comes!" Hawg shouted. "Get the net! Get the net!"

I slipped the net over the side, expecting that at best Hawg had tied into a big, sluggish sucker. Despite Hawg's euphoria, all the action was in our boat. The surface of the lake looked as calm and serene as the old-timer's expression. Hawg cranked away at his reel; the drag sounded as if he were trying to lift a Greyhound bus from the bottom of the lake. Just then a slimy, muck-covered log broke the surface. Hawg's chocolate-scented worm was wrapped around one end.

"Figures," the old man said. "Them flashy-looking fake worms with the slip sinkers are always getting snagged on something. Best way to fish this lake is with a cane pole and a live nightcrawler. These fish have seen so many durn fakes they forgot what a real worm looks like. Toss in a live one and the bass go plum wild."

Hawg stared at his catch. He didn't seem to know whether to cry or cuss.

"How about you?" I asked the old-timer. "You have any luck?"

"I kept a few small ones," he said. The old man reached over the far side of his skiff and pulled a stringer from the water. Five big largemouths glistened in the sunlight. The smallest looked as big as a boat cushion.

"Geez!" I said. "Jest look at them *pigs*!"

The old man looked at me and shook his head. "Must be contagious, huh?" he asked.

Hawg worked his way to the bow of the bassfinder rig, struggling with the snag. The old-timer said goodbye and rowed off with his catch. I ran back to the outboard.

"Well, you about ready to call it a day?" Hawg asked.

"*Hail*, no," I told him. "I'm a-gonna go back out. Didn't you see the porkers that old coot was carrying?"

Hawg blinked at me. "But we don't have any nightcrawlers."

"No, but we can run into town and pick up a box. Might not hurt to pick up a couple of cane poles, too."

"Yeah," said Hawg, still trying to save his plastic worm, "maybe we can even find an old duck skiff to rent."

I grabbed the outboard's throttle. "Cut the string on that eel'n'jig, will ya?" I told Hawg. "Day's a'wastin'."

I opened the outboard's throttle and the bassfinder rig leaped from the water as it rocketed into space, nearly spilling Hawg from his throne.

"Hang on, boy!" I called to him. "We're gonna nail us some frogs—and I mean *bodacious*!"

TWENTY-ONE

A Sportsman's Lifetime Reading List

I'm always eager to improve my hunting and fishing skills, and so I frequently buy books to learn more about the outdoors.

The curriculum has been brutal.

A Guide to Reading Trout Water was just as hard to read as trout water was in the first place.

A Beginner's Guide to Waterfowling wasn't much help, either. Maybe the author can set out decoys in a perfect J-pattern, but my best efforts look like scattered M & M's.

A Field Guide to the Stars is a good read if you like humor. How else do you explain the ancient Greeks' insistence that the constellations resemble beasts?

"Eureka!" shouts Archimedes. "Let's call that bunch of stars 'Taurus.' We'll tell everyone it resembles a bull."

"That's a good one," cries Plato, howling with laughter. "Centuries from now people will wonder whether we saw a bull or if we were slinging it."

Although I know that's the way most field guides evolve, I continue to buy them, compulsively. If field guides were bourbon, I'd be the town drunk. Just yesterday I found an old knapsack I'd forgotten about; inside was my copy of *A Field Guide to*

Natural Baits—along with a mummified leech and some petrified grubs.

A Guide to Walleye Fishing contains my favorite recipe for shore lunch. It consists of golden-brown walleye filets, seasoned fried potatoes, and a salad of fresh-picked wintercress and juneberries. I've been lugging that book around in the bottom of my tackle box for years; so far, my most elaborate shore lunch has been a pinch of Copenhagen.

I've always had a talent for getting turned around in the woods. I thought I had solved the problem when I purchased a GPS unit, but for some reason changing the batteries never occurs to me. As a safety precaution I read *Basic Orienteering* to learn how to use a map and compass, but I got lost between "Triangulation" and "Hypsosographic Features." My idea of basic orienteering is using terms like: "I think the road is over there."

Terminology is always confusing when it comes to outdoor nomenclature. Last spring I decided to learn something about forecasting weather—I thought it'd be a good idea, since I've been surprised by storms while fishing far from shore. I purchased a copy of *A Practical Guide to Meteorology* and tried to memorize everything I needed to know about cirrus, cirrostratus, altostratus, stratocumulus, nimbostratus, and cumulus clouds. The next time I need to forecast weather, I'll listen to the radio.

Another problem with books is that they leave large gaps in the knowledge they impart—which can make you look stupid when you're trying to impress someone. You need quick wits if some smart aleck bully starts hectoring you about your facts. This happened to me last summer, when the eight-year-old girl from a neighboring campsite wandered over to visit.

"What kind of loon is that one, Mister?" she asked.

"A common loon," I told her.

"How do you know?"

"I know because they're pretty common on this lake."

"Why is it quacking? Loons are supposed to *yodel*."

"Say, aren't those your parents packing up and driving away?"

Guidebooks to specific places are always suspect. I guess the idea of actually visiting the places they're writing about never occurs to the authors. *A Canoeist's Guide to the Chikonchit River* is a good example. My wife and I decided to run the river this spring, after the book promised that "the Chikonchit's easy rapids should cause no problems for novices in open canoes."

I couldn't even see our canoe as the current plunged us into the whitewater cauldron of Hell's Rapids—I'd already shut my eyes back at Dead Man's Falls. Water crashed over our gunwales from every side as Peg paddled frantically to keep us afloat—but it was hopeless. She looked over her shoulder at me.

"We're gonna die! We're gonna die! Make a jump for it!"

"Shut up and stay in the canoe!"

It was terrible, seeing someone you love go to pieces like that. To Peg's credit, she's been nice enough not to tease me about it.

TWENTY-TWO

Deercampsia Hypomnesia

Psychologists have reported evidence of a previously unrecognized psychological phenomenon: *Deercampsia Hypomnesia.* Clinical observations characterize it as a state of "perpetual and inexplicable forgetfulness." Oddly enough, this malady manifests itself in only two distinct groups of people—institutionalized amnesiacs and deer hunters.

I don't know about institutionalized amnesiacs, but the discovery of a "perpetual and inexplicable" state of forgetfulness afflicting deer hunters comes as no surprise. I could have told the shrinks about it years ago, if only I'd remembered.

During the forty years that I've hunted deer, I have, at one time or another, forgotten about everything from back tags to bullets. And on one occasion, while attending the Saturday night festivities at the Deerhunters' Ball in Hurley (Sin City), Wisconsin, I was even accused of forgetting my name and the fact that I was married.

During this same period of time, I've observed that my hunting partners are also regularly stricken by an inexplicable forgetfulness, especially when it comes to returning gear that they borrowed or repaying funds that I loaned them for a poker stake.

Indeed, whereas many of my deer camp companions go by nicknames such as "Buck," "Stump Sitter," "Double-Ought Dick," or "Deadeye," I am rudely referred to as "Bank of America."

Their insolence—and my absentmindedness—was one reason why, a few years back, I tried my hand at hunting alone. Inexplicably, I've forgotten nothing about that incident.

After parking the 4 × 4 at the end of a rabbit run (the map referred to it as an "unimproved road"), and then hiking ten miles into the woods with enough gear strapped to my back to outfit all the deer camps in Upper Michigan, I discovered that I had left my only box of cartridges on the kitchen table, 400 miles away, in the bag of gear I was sure I would never need. I spent that opening day trying to find shells at every gun shop within a 40-mile radius of my camp, before finally locating what must have been the last box of .38-40 loads in the county.

"Not the county," the shopkeeper told me, "but the *state*. Incidentally, if you want them, it'll cost you fifty bucks."

"Fifty dollars? For a box of shells?" I couldn't remember anyone—not even my usual hunting partners—ever taking such brazen advantage of me.

"Hey, what can I say?" the shopkeeper said. "It's opening day, you're 400 miles from home, and I've got the only box of factory-loaded .38-40 slugs on this side of the *universe*. I've got to make a little profit; after all, a box of .38-40's is about as rare as a deer hunter with a good memory."

After that experience, I became a firm believer in making lists and checking off each item whenever I packed my gear for camp. Never again, I vowed, would I forget the bullets. As a fail-safe measure, I even retired my .38-40 and purchased a brand-new .30-30. Experience had taught me that there are more boxes of .30-30 shells sitting on the hardware store shelves of the Northwoods than there are people on Earth. But I was to learn that forgetting the ammo was only one of the symptoms of *Deercampsia Hypomnesia.*

* * *

Last season, while preparing for the ride up to camp, I was confident that every item I might conceivably need was securely stowed in the back of the 4 × 4. I had my list, checked it twice, and I would have bet a full, $50 box of .38-40 shells that I hadn't forgotten a thing. Yet, just as I was pulling out of the driveway at dawn, I saw my wife dash out of the house and sprint across the lawn in her robe. I slammed on the brakes, fearing that the house had caught fire; but it proved to be something that my wife felt was far more catastrophic. I'd forgotten to leave her the checkbook.

Fortunately, I didn't forget my way to the cabin, and that evening, during the rituals traditionally observed on the first night in deer camp, I even remembered that a flush will always beat a straight. I also remembered to get into bed before sunrise, and by the time 4 A.M. arrived, I believed I was on a roll (for once, I even remembered to pack an alarm clock).

But my euphoria was to be short-lived. I wanted to be on my stand before legal shooting hours began at dawn, and I planned on leaving the cabin an hour before sunrise. My reasoning was that it would take me twenty minutes to walk through the woods in the dark to my stand, twenty minutes to get myself situated and comfortable, and another twenty minutes to let my eyes grow accustomed to the change in light. And so, wishing good luck to the others, I stepped out into a predawn November morning that was as black and cold as the cabin's woodstove (someone had forgotten to get up in the middle of the night to stoke the coals).

I pulled the flashlight from my pocket and flicked on the switch. I'd remembered the flashlight, all right—it was No. 2 on my list, just below "shells" and just above "toilet paper." But I had forgotten to add something like "check batteries" to the roster. The result was one corroded and useless flashlight.

Forty-five minutes later, it was apparent that I'd also forgotten how to find the way to my stand in the dark. After spending the better part of an hour playing blind-man's bluff in a hazelbrush thicket, I had to admit that I was lost (my list didn't include a compass because I never need one), and that if I didn't choose someplace quick to stand, I'd still be wandering around when the sun came up. In the end, I picked a tangle of windfalls along a ridgetop overlooking a swamp.

I crawled through the maze of roots and branches, and as soon as I was comfortably situated among them, my metabolic processes reminded me that I had forgotten to do something important before leaving camp. This, undoubtedly, is one of the most classic symptoms of *Deercampsia Hypomnesia.* There must be some immutable, cosmic law that dictates nature will not call on a deer hunter until he is on his stand in the middle of a subzero woods, swaddled in long johns, two pairs of pants, and a fluorescent-orange jumpsuit with a stuck zipper. Unable to resist the call, I climbed back out of the windfalls to answer. It was then I discovered that item No. 3 on my list was back at camp.

* * *

The first shots of the season echoed in the distance as I crawled back inside the windfalls. I slipped a half-dozen shells into the tubular magazine of my lever-action .30-30, and began my yearly ritual of trying to remain still for more than three seconds at a time.

There's another, little-known cosmic law that states the temperature will always drop a minimum of 40 degrees as soon as a deer hunter tries to remain motionless on his stand. And one of the symptoms of *Deercampsia Hypomnesia* is that the deer hunter always forgets this.

I began to shake. I began to shuffle. I began stamping my feet to keep my toes from becoming ice cubes. The hairs on my mustache turned stiff and white with ice, while I chastised myself for forgetting to add things like "thermos/hot coffee," "handwarmers," or even a simple "gloves" to my list.

When my hands began turning the color of birchbark, I realized that frostbite could be a real threat. Remembering what I had read about outdoor survival, I laid the gun aside, opened my jumpsuit, and jammed my fingers under my arms. Unfortunately, I failed to remember that other cosmic law of deer hunting: If you want to see a deer, lean your gun against a tree.

The brush cracked off to my left, and out of the corner of my eye I saw the phantasmagoric shape of a deer. I held my breath and went still as a rock. It was one of the biggest whitetails I had ever seen, with a rack that belonged on an elk. It was standing broadside to me, less than 100 yards from my knocking knees, without so much as a cobweb to obstruct the view. It was the classic shot I had always dreamed about and, quite classically, my rifle was three feet away.

The buck was feeding on acorns, and I decided to go for the gun the next time he lowered his head to feed. I was confident I could make the shot.

Suddenly the buck's head snapped erect. His front hooves pawed the ground while twin jets of steam snorted from his nostrils. He was on to me, and in a moment he would bolt. Without having to think about it, I went for the gun, threw it against my shoulder, laid the iron sights across the deer's chest, and pulled back the hammer, all in one, fluid, effortless motion. I was poetry in pac boots as I squeezed the trigger.

Click.

The sound of the empty gun sent the buck bounding away through the brush. I'd remembered to fill the gun's magazine, all right—but I'd forgotten to crank the lever to feed a shell into the chamber. I watched as the deer's white flag disappeared over the next ridge. Ten seconds later, a single rifle shot shattered the silence. Then a familiar voice cried out: "I got him! I got him! I got him!"

My kid brother, Bubba, was standing over the deer when I walked up on him a few minutes later.

"Hey, Bank of America!" he called when he saw me. "Do you have any idea at all where we are? I got turned around in the dark when I was lookin' for my stand this morning."

I nodded at his trophy. "You know, that should have been my deer," I said.

"Oh, yeah? Then why didn't you shoot him?"

"*Deercampsia Hypomnesia,*" I told him.

"Huh?"

"Perpetual and inexplicable forgetfulness."

"Yeah, well, with your luck I'm surprised you even remember what a deer looks like."

I ignored the remark. "That's a nice buck you got there, kiddo. He'll top 200 pounds, easy. You want a hand with him?"

"Sure," said Bubba, "but let me have your knife so I can tag him." He held out his open palm.

"What's wrong with your knife?" I asked.

"Nothing. I honed it all last night and it's razor-sharp. But it's back at the cabin. I forgot it along with the rope."

Rope? Quickly I made a mental note to add that item to my list.

Suddenly Bubba let out with an agonizing howl, while his hands flailed away at the small of his back. "Oh, no!" he groaned. The words were a theatrical gasp. "I don't believe this!"

"What's wrong? Are you all right?"

"It's my back," Bubba said. He showed me his clenched teeth. They may have been holding back his pain, but I could swear I saw a smile. "My back just went out on me—just like *that.*" He snapped his fingers. "I can't bend down to gut my deer; and I won't be able to drag it back to camp, wherever that is. Would you mind doing those things for me? *Please*?"

"Are you serious?" I asked.

He winced. "I think you'll have to carry my gun, too."

"But your back hasn't bothered you in years," I told him.

He smiled at me, and something in his grin reminded me of the shopkeeper who had sold me those .38-40 shells years before.

"I know," Bubba said. "I forgot."

TWENTY-THREE

Sports Show

I look forward to the spring sport show as eagerly as a kid waiting for Christmas. Its arrival is greeted with more hoopla than if the president were coming to town. By the time the caravan of travel trailers pulls in at the convention center, I'll be flush with all the urgency of a spawning salmon. Here—between the flyfishing exhibits and the salesmen hawking gizmo knives—I launch the year's first foray into conspicuous consumption.

Like a moth lured to a lantern, I'm drawn to the dazzling displays of reels and rods, lures and tackle, boats and motors, and all the other paraphernalia that promises to make me a better fisherman—for a price.

I already own a dozen spinning and bait-casting outfits—not including my flyfishing gear, cane poles, and tip-ups. My wife hasn't bought a new dress in years and my son's orthodontist is threatening debtor's prison; obviously, what our family really needs is a pack rod.

I truly believe a new pack rod—complete with carrying case, spinning reel, and a spare spool of line—will make next season the kind of season I'll remember for a lifetime. My wife, Peg, wants to know why I can't remember the fishing seasons

I've already experienced, especially since most of them are still reflected in the unpaid balance on my credit cards.

I like the travel brochures from fishing lodges that set up camp downstream of the inflatable canoes and vacuum cleaner salesman. I like the heft of a plastic shopping bag stuffed with leaflets touting fly-in trips to the Arctic, or vacations aboard houseboats that make the house I live in seem like a shed.

I like the pretty girls who dole out free samples of organic trail mix, or the ones clad in Spandex who cast a "come hither" smile while straddling a jet ski. They know I'm an easy mark and I know it, too, so it's a good thing I don't have room for a jet ski. On the other hand, Peg recently cleared up a lot of space in our kitchen cupboards. Would anyone like a case of vintage organic trail mix? I'm told 1998 was a very good year.

I like the makeshift plastic swimming pools filled with hatchery trout who are just as snooty as their wild cousins. I like the ratty fiberglass rods you use to try and catch them, while tossing a fly that looks like a shuttlecock. I like the excited squeal of a youngster when her dad yells, "Fish on!" and the serious, single guys who fish the swimming pool as deliberately as if they were on the Madison. I like the old-timers who complain about the conditions even though we're fishing indoors. And I like the slack-jawed little kids who peer down at the fish as if the trout were gold coins in a wishing well. After all this time, I still remember the magic.

Someday Peg would like to buy one of those luxurious, sport show campers—the ones with microwaves, stereo-surround systems, TV, and a tub. Peg claims she'd enjoy fishing a lot more if she could sleep on a queen-size bed in an air-conditioned camper. But until my income equals my outgo, we'll have to make do with our tent. It may not have a tub, but in a downpour we do have running water.

I like the stage shows featuring rock groups that were popular when I was still young enough to hear the music. I like the dog tricks, the lumberjack shows, and the stand-up comics from places like Fargo. I don't even mind being plucked from the audience and humiliated onstage by a magician who pulls silk hankies from my ears.

For some reason, bratwurst tastes better at a sport show. To be sure, the beer is always colder. And although I resent finding another angler on a stream and consider him a crowd, I enjoy being part of the happy throng of folks who swarm the aisles of a sport show. It's a bit like casting a line and landing a prize fish whenever I spot an old friend among the faces.

I like the look of surprise when he sees me, his eagerness to catch up on our lives, and reminiscing about fishing trips that were too few and long ago. Sometimes, we'll head over to the indoor beer garden with my bag of brochures to make new plans. And maybe, in spring, we'll get together on a stream not far from home and remember why fishing has more to do with friendship than fish.

For all the glitter and gadgets and downright silliness that is a sport show, there's no place I'd rather be when lakes and streams are thawing, but opening day is still weeks away. Look for me at the virtual fishing exhibit when the marlin are running—I'll be the guy with a mouthful of trail mix and silk hankies dangling from his ears.

TWENTY-FOUR

Mr. Majestik

Aldo Leopold once said there were two kinds of hunting: ordinary hunting and ruffed grouse hunting.

He might also have mentioned that there are two kinds of hunters: ordinary hunters and megalomaniacs.

Bubba, my hunting partner, is one of the megalomaniacs. Aside from fancying himself the greatest outdoorsman since Leatherstocking, he drives a pickup truck emblazoned with the giant logo: Mr. Majestik.

"It's an apt name for a man of my talents," Bubba said. "And how about that lettering job—nice, huh? Bet you'd never guess I did it myself."

In addition to being a lousy speller and a megalomaniac, Mr. Majestik is also my kid brother. The family claims he's only a young man trying to prove himself to an older brother. That's easy for them to say—they don't have a hunting cabin in northern Wisconsin. If home is where they have to take you in, then my cabin is home to Mr. Majestik. Come autumn, I can usually find His Majesty at my cabin any day of the week: After spending half of his life skipping classes at college, Mr. Majestik has made a career out of looking for a job.

"Yeah, I can usually get away anytime," Bubba will say. "Too bad, though, I couldn't get away to help when you were building this dump. If I had, this shack would be something you could brag about."

Admittedly, no self-respecting person likes to think of himself as being "average," and that's especially true when it comes to outdoor skills. But Bubba's ego totters at the edge of dementia.

Once, when we were invited guests at a sporting lodge, I watched Bubba and our host put up a pair of woodcock. Both men fired twice, simultaneously. Our host dropped the birds. Bubba bagged a tree.

"That was incredible shooting!" Bubba said. "Not one man in a million can double on woodcock like that."

Our host was pleased by the remark until Bubba turned to him and asked, "Why didn't you take a shot?"

Strangers who hunt with Bubba for the first time rarely return for a second loathsome encounter. Yet even if we weren't related, I'd still include Mr. Majestik among my friends. Maybe it's because I've never gotten the hang of giving up hope. In the same way I can't bear to rid myself of a favorite reel that has lost more than a few screws, I can't bring myself to part with Bubba. I like to think that someday the missing pieces will turn up, and I'll no longer need to make excuses for harboring Bubba and other seemingly useless junk.

My kid brother's delusions of grandeur would be easier to tolerate if there were any truth to his claims, but after years of roaming the woods with him, I know better.

As sagas go, Bubba's "big buck" story comes close to rivaling the *Iliad* and the *Odyssey* for epic proportions. He tells about "stalking the demon beast through the killing cold" and how he got close enough to the animal to see "the fires of hell in its man-hating eyes." Bubba makes mention of "slashing horns and well-honed hooves" and holds his audience breathless as he describes how "the enraged behemoth charged like a legion of devils gone wild." By the time Bubba finishes telling his tale, you're never sure whether he was hunting or witnessing an exorcism.

Bubba's liberality with facts extends to his tracking skills as well.

"See that?" he'll ask, pointing to one of several thousand deer prints in the snow. "I'd say five does and a yearling spike passed this way at sunup. There's an old mosshorn with them, too. He goes about 235 pounds with a 14-point rack, and I can tell by the way the track is splayed that this is his seventh winter."

In a duckblind, Bubba is quick to critique a shot. If we each take a bird from the same speeding flock of bluebills, his will be the one that "came streaking in over the blind like a bottle rocket," while my duck dropped out of the sky only because His Majesty "made an assist." And on those occasions when Bubba misses a shot, he never fails to assess blame.

"Damn," he'll mutter, staring up into space, "that's the last time I'll use those crummy reloads of yours."

Our relationship was put to the test last year during the final day of deer season. The worst November blizzard in thirty years dumped two feet of snow on Wisconsin within a few hours, and hunters all across the North were finding themselves stranded in the woods. I suggested to Bubba that we forget about trying to fill our tags and stay in camp instead.

"Ha! That's just what I'd expect from an ordinary hunter," Bubba told me. "Soon as the weather turns the least bit bad, you go to pieces and want to stay in camp."

"Bubba, the radio said that weather conditions today are *life-threatening*. Doesn't that mean anything to you?"

"It sure does! It means you and all the other crybabies will be staying indoors, so I'll have the woods to myself. Mr. Majestik never gives up—I ain't comin' back till I get my buck!"

That was at six in the morning. Ten hours later, Bubba had yet to return. Much as I hate to admit it, I was worried about His Majesty. What if something had happened? What if he had gotten into trouble and couldn't get back? Bubba was out there, alone, in a blizzard, and I had let him go. The thought of that turned my concern to guilt. What kind of man would abandon his brother? What kind of friend would let his buddy hunt alone in a storm? So what if Mr. Majestik was a jerk? He was *my* jerk, my baby brother.

Just before dark I got into my woolens, took down the snowshoes, and headed for the place where Bubba usually takes a stand at dusk.

The snow was waist-deep in the open places, and the biting wind felt like it was ripping the flesh from my face. But that was nothing compared to my unexpected swim in the Brule River. It was here that I tumbled down a thirty-foot bluff after bulldozing my way through a hazelbrush thicket. I was cold, wet, frozen, and numb, and my waterproof matches were back at the cabin. If Bubba wasn't in poor shape when I found him, I'd make sure he'd be hurting before we got back to camp.

I met a hunter on the logging trail that led to Bubba's stand, and asked him for a match.

"Sorry, but I left my matches back up this trail a mile or so," the hunter said. "A fella there's got himself a nice little spikehorn; I gave him my matches so he could have a fire for company. I offered to help drag his deer out, but he said his big, dumb brother would be coming by to look for him. He said he'd let his brother drag out the buck."

"What did this guy look like?" I asked.

"Can't say what he looks like," the hunter said, "but he sounded like he was hallucinating. I think he was trying to tell me how he shot his deer, but all I got out of it was some gibberish about devils and demons and charging behemoths."

The sense of relief came over me like a flood. "Yep! That's Bubba, all right," I said.

"Bubba? No, that wasn't his name," the hunter replied. "This guy told me he was Mr. Majestik."

PART FOUR

HOME FROM THE HILL

TWENTY-FIVE

A Place in the Woods

The cabin sits at the end of a narrow dirt road, on a hill above tiny Lucerne Lake. In this corner of northwest Wisconsin—where there is almost as much water as land—Lucerne is one of the many thousands of lakes that lie within the St. Croix River's watershed.

I built the cabin years ago, in the way cabins used to be built: posts and beams; boards and battens; shakes and shims and stones. It stands among the jackpines as if it had always been there, as weathered and timeworn as a cedar. Just big enough for one or two friends and whatever gear we can carry, I built it as a getaway.

I live in a town not far from the cabin. The town is where I work, tend my family, pay my bills, help my neighbors, and try to contribute to the common good. But when the press of responsibilities is more than I can bear, I escape to the woods. The cabin is my anchor-hold—its dependable familiarity keeps me rooted against the currents of inconstancy. Here, where time is changeless, the past and its memories are as near as yesterday. Insulated by silence, the cabin's solitudes shelter me from the hurried and the hectic. The town is where I live, but the cabin is where I belong.

* * *

In April, when the snow is all but gone and frozen lakes lie shattered with open leads of blue water, I return to the cabin to prepare for all that is to come. There are floors to sweep, mice to evict, a pump to prime, and tomorrows to dream about.

Days are growing longer as the sun climbs higher, and warm winds are flush with the scent of balsam and pine. The incessant patter of trickling snowmelt makes every brook roar like a torrent. Sunny cowslips are already blooming along muddy banks, and at night clamoring flocks of geese pass unseen through the dark. Killdeer are keening. Pike are spawning. And everywhere is a sense of quickening. Winter is receding and life is unfolding as the advancing tide of spring returns.

April is the season of expectations. I spend its first days patching waders, repairing canoes, and checking tackle. Alone at the cabin in April, I'm as free as a boy—and just as ready for adventure. I might decide to fish for crappies in a creek brimming with snowmelt; or maybe I'll try for steelhead in the rivers that tumble north to Lake Superior. Or I may go exploring to discover what the vanishing snow has revealed, and return with a pine knot or deer skull—objects with a past as unfathomable to me as spring's resurrection. I watch seagulls cartwheel and eagles soar while splitting wood for the evening's fire. At night, when the fire burns brightly behind the glass door of the cabin's stove, I settle back and dream.

This will be the year I land "Big Bertha," the 8-pound bass that haunts the shadows under my dock; I've had that fish on twice before, and twice I've watched it spit my plug. This will also be the year I hit Popple Creek at the same time the woodcock do—and this year I'll remember the hip boots. This year I won't miss the salmon run on the Amnicon, and I'll wait for a trophy buck instead of bagging a spike-horn for the freezer.

In April, anything is possible.

Soon friends will gather at the cabin and in the days ahead we'll share trout streams, johnboats, duck blinds, and deer stands—and then reality will intrude with empty creels and unused tags. But in April the cabin is my middle-aged version of a tree house where I'm free to be a boy again; a boy who—despite all the broken promises of the past—still believes in the dreams of spring.

* * *

Summer is the season of abundance, when life is easy and carefree. I live at the cabin from the time the loon chicks hatch until the teal flee south in late August.

This far north, summer is a long time in coming. It doesn't arrive until after Father's Day, when the bass move off their spawning beds. By then the air is thick with insects, and the bright blue flags of wild irises wave like showy emblems along lakeshores. The summer people have returned to their cabins and during the day the lake bustles with activity: kids dive from rafts or catch sunfish from docks; men in canoes hunt pike and perch.

By July my cabin has long been a base camp for friends. By then we've made dozens of fishing forays into the surrounding woods: rainbows on the Sioux; browns on the Clam; walleyes and pike on the Totagatic and Namekagon; smallmouths on the St. Croix; muskies on the Chippewa; and brookies in every beaver pond.

During the long and lush green days of summer, it's easy to believe the freewheeling atmosphere will last forever. The woods teem with blueberries free for the picking; juneberry trees sag with the weight of their fruit. Bluegills cluster around the ends of piers, and on the lake flocks of young ducks move about like armadas. The dusk is filled with the warbling of finches and after sunset flying squirrels glide through the trees. Through it all winds the trembling calls of the loons, a quavering, wistful tolling that seems to ask: *Who are you*?

Most of the summer people give up on cabin life when August arrives: temperatures soar; the sun bakes exposed flesh; and lakes are thick with weeds and suspended matter. Biting flies and clouds of mosquitoes drive even the most resilient people off the water. But for me, the serious fishing is just beginning.

In August, when the sunset's afterglow has burned away and swarms of insects rattle the cabin's screens, I bathe in DEET, pull on sneakers and cut-off jeans, and go down to the lake with a Hula Popper. I wade the shallows up to my waist, testing each step with a toe, mindful of the submerged beaver slash and muskrat runs that make these shallows the kind of place where largemouths lurk on summer evenings.

At night, the sound of bass feeding on the topwater is as noisy as a youngster slurping soup. When the fish jump they splash like otters. I cast to the edge of lily pads and pickerelweeds, letting the popper lie motionless while I watch shooting stars streak across the sky. At the north end of the lake, loons are yodeling. Bats dart over the water, so near I instinctively wave them away, a little concerned that their sonar might fail and I'll end up with a bat in my face.

These soft, summer nights are among my favorite at the cabin. Maybe it's because they remind me of other summer evenings, long ago. When I was a kid my father and I fished for walleyes on summer evenings during his annual, week-long vacation; on other nights I'd fish for bullheads and catfish with friends. We were kids, without worries or commitments, and sometimes we'd stay out until dawn, huddling around the light of a driftwood fire, occasionally dozing off on a bed of long grass and spruce boughs. Every one of those summers was a tintype copy of the last; it never occurred to us that things might ever be different.

These are the thoughts that keep me company as I prowl for bass on summer evenings. After the Hula Popper has laid at rest for a time, I begin its slow and sputtering retrieve. Almost before I complete a full turn of the reel's handle, a largemouth bursts from under the lily pads and inhales the popper.

Most of the bass are decent size; one or two would look respectable on a wall—but all go back. I'm just getting the kinks out, I tell myself. My real quarry is Big Bertha, the 8-pound monster under my dock.

I make my meandering way toward the dock and plant my sneakers in the lake's sandy bottom when I'm within two dozen feet of the pier. At night I never risk long casts: there's too much out there to snag and entangle the evening in frustration. I cast the popper near the end of the dock; when I start my retrieve, a bass as big as a small dog wallops the lure.

The fish jumps, twice, but I don't need to see it to know it's Big Bertha. The drag of the spinning reel squeals. I keep the rod up, trying to turn the fish away from the pickerelweeds. Soon the bass is almost within reach, offering no more resistance than an anchor. And then suddenly, inexplicably, and without warning, the bass explodes like a torpedo and spits the popper into the air. The fish is gone. Big Bertha has humbled me again. But then, if I had caught her, summer would be over. And I'm in no hurry to say goodbye to the easy luxuriance and abundance that is summer.

"Take all the swift advantage of the hours," wrote Shakespeare, and that's what I do at the cabin during the few and fleeting days of summer. This far north, summer arrives late and leaves early; almost before you know it is there, it is gone.

* * *

Autumn is the shortest season in the North. By Labor Day, the teal are gone and the rose-breasted grosbeaks have vanished. Wild rice beds grow sere and soundless while the woods burst into riotous colors: flaming reds, tangerine-orange, lemon-yellows. Tamaracks smolder like smoky gold in the swamps and in the morning flocks of ringbills sail down into potholes. By noon the sun has burned away the frost and snipe break from the bulrushes. At dusk woodcock careen through the birches.

October used to drive me crazy when I was younger. There was too much to chase and never enough hours for pursuit. Until Columbus Day, there were too many leaves on the trees to hunt grouse; and then the leaves would drop, the steelhead would return, pike began to bite, and bluebills came hurtling out of the sky. I wanted to do and have it all, but there was never enough time. Two weeks later snow would fall, lakes would freeze, and autumn was suddenly over.

Fifty years ago the outdoor writer, Gordon MacQuarrie, had a cabin not far from mine and wrote about the dilemma: "How would you like to hole up in a country where you could choose, as you fell asleep, between duck hunting and partridge hunting, between small-mouths on a good river like the St. Croix or trout on another good one like the Brule, or between muskie fishing on the Chippewa flowage or cisco dipping in the dark for the fun of it?"

Not much has changed since MacQuarrie roamed these woods, except perhaps for my thinking. Like the dun-colored days and pewter skies of early November, a certain maturity has finally settled in.

In autumn, at the cabin, I'm made keenly aware that life is not so much a journey as it is a pursuit. It begins as a search for who we are before the chase begins for the things we desire. The lucky few among us—if we survive our mistakes—eventually learn that the real prize is not the quarry but the quest. The quest is life and living; everything else is straw.

Contentment is the most elusive of quarries. For me, it was as long in coming as the first flock of bluebills. It was always there, like birds in a thicket, but I never knew it until I discovered satisfaction in the small and trifling things I do at the cabin: chopping wood; waiting for the weather; going for long, aimless walks with the dog and a gun simply to enjoy wasting time. I no longer need or want it all because—to my way of thinking—I already have a lot; and a lot is more than enough. And because I've come to understand this, I consider myself among the most fortunate of men.

Autumn is the season of thanksgiving.

* * *

Winter arrives in November just before deer season. It begins as a hush, as if November were holding its breath, before a rustling sound stirs the brown and lifeless woods, and the air becomes white with swirling flakes. The coarse, crystalline snow settles onto logs and leaves and frozen lakes, covering the landscape in a colorless cloak. Within an hour, autumn is a memory. Now begins the long, inanimate, and alabaster abeyance that is winter, the season of resignation.

In late November, friends and family gather at the cabin for deer camp: sons and fathers, brothers and uncles; nephews and cousins, old friends and new faces. A cabin that was meant to sleep three people is suddenly home to a dozen. After a week, it can get to be too much of a good thing. Yet, when the last deer is taken down from the meat pole, and the caravan of pickup trucks winds its way back along the twin ruts of the snowy road away from the cabin, the solitude with which I'm left is not as companionable as I remember.

In winter I'm usually alone at the cabin except for the squirrels and mice and weasels. On warm days when sun dogs play above the horizon, I'll set out tip-ups on the ice for pike, or take the snowshoes and shotgun in search of white rabbits—"varying hares," the Canadians call them.

Some nights I watch the northern lights blaze below Polaris, while the frozen lake booms and groans with the sound of expanding ice. At midnight, aspens explode as if rent with dynamite as the temperature plunges to thirty below zero. I feel alone in an arctic landscape where every element is extinguishing life. And then, from back in the dark timber, the night's wintry isolation is pierced by a mournful howl—a low, deep-throated wailing that makes the goose flesh swarm over my arms.

The timber wolves trot in a straight line down the center of the lake, their tails pointing straight out behind them. The snow reflects the light of the moon, and the scene is illuminated in shades of royal blue and ivory. I'm safe in my cabin, but the deer have no shelter; and in the morning the snow will tell a tale of death in the woods.

But for me, the lucky one, there will be another tomorrow, with wood to split, fish to catch, trails to tramp, and long nights in front of the fire for dreaming. And that, I suppose, is the reason for the cabin. I built it as a getaway, only to discover I wasn't fleeing anything at all. Instead, I was running toward something: toward mystery, beauty, wonder, and joy—toward life, and the adventure it was meant to be.

TWENTY-SIX

Mementos

My wife is one of those people who abhors clutter, whether it be the stacks of outdoor magazines and catalogues lying next to my recliner, or the personal baggage we lug from one stage of our lives to the next—the dreams and plans and hoped for reconciliations that will never happen but are too dear to forget.

Lately she's been rifling our house, weeding through the refuse, looking for things to sell at her next rummage sale. Among the items she has scavenged is a trout knife I tried to fashion from an old milling file—a knife that never really shed its scrap iron origins. She's also unearthed the first pair of binoculars I ever owned, an army surplus model that saw service in the Punic Wars.

I'm wise enough to let Peg have her way with these things, but I put my foot down when I discovered an ancient hollow-steel rod with a level-wind bait-casting reel of dubious vintage lying on the rubble heap of my personal history. It's an heirloom I used to snatch from my father's garage when I was a boy.

Admittedly, it wasn't an heirloom back then—I was just a kid who used his dad's gear to go fishing—but I borrowed it often enough to think of it as mine, and time has given the rod a quality that is irreplaceable. I haven't cast a plug with it since

Kennedy was president, but whenever I see that steel rod and its reel of black braided-cotton line, I'm twelve years old again, hurling a Bass-Oreno across the untroubled waters of Wilson's Pond, confident that things would never change, and that life's biggest hurdle was landing a bass before supper.

"You can't sell this," I told Peg, retrieving the treasure.

"You haven't looked at that rod in years. It's junk."

"It's a memento," I corrected.

"What's the difference?"

There is a difference, but explaining it to a person who has a fetish for ridding the world of clutter is like explaining Pascal's Wager to a cynic. Still, our little exchange has gotten me to thinking about my collection of souvenirs, and why some items are keepsakes while others are clearly junk.

* * *

Mementos are what we make them. For whatever reason, a particular object—often of no real value—becomes imbued with our affection for a place or time we were reluctant to leave, and to which we would gladly return. We try and keep the memory alive in a bit of fool's gold pocketed from a Colorado trout stream, or a pinecone tucked away during a trip to the Maine woods. Mementos such as these recapture the past and resurrect the contentment we knew.

This is certainly true of my collection of small stones. When the composer, Frédéric Chopin, left his imprisoned Poland to live in exile, he took along a tiny urn of Polish soil so as to never be completely separated from the land he loved. Later, when he died in France, the urn was buried with Chopin in a Paris cemetery. For much the same reason, I've been carting around an old coffee can filled with stones.

I've plucked the pebbles from trout streams, campsites, and similar places that hold significance for me. These were places where I once spent a lot of time, and where I was as happy as I ever expected to be. Even now I'd give much to revisit those haunts; but time has altered some of them, and others are in distant places I'm not apt to soon see. But my memories of those places are forever stored in the stones I keep in a battered coffee can. I doubt I'll be as romantic as Chopin and ask to be buried with my pebbles—but I might. If I do, look in the closet behind the box on the shelf—the box that contains my lifetime collection of old hunting licenses.

* * *

There's a different story behind the three partridge tails I keep displayed on a shelf. They come from a stand of staghorn sumac along Upper Michigan's Montreal River, and the day I flushed three grouse at once. Since then, my reflexes are a bit less than quick, and lately I've taken to shooting behind the birds when they explode from October's forest duff. But the fantails on my shelf remind me of when I once did the impossible and dropped three birds with three shells from a double-gun.

There's an old Swedish knife I keep in my desk. The cheap wood handle split and was lost years ago while cleaning pike along the Kenogami River, not far from James Bay. I bought the knife at a Hudson Bay store on my first trip to the Canadian bush—back when I fancied myself a seasoned outdoorsman, even though I was too young to shave. Over the years I've used that knife for everything from picking my teeth and butchering venison to filleting perch and whittling tent stakes.

Once—when I was alone and barely out of my teens—I plunged through the ice of a frozen lake. I rescued myself by holding the knife like an ice pick and driving it into the lake ice so that I could pull myself free of the frigid water. It saved me.

Knives are made of better steel today, and they don't come with cheap, wooden handles dipped in red paint. But when I open the desk, searching for stamps, and spot that broken knife lying among the paperclips and pencils, I remember when the North was new and unknown to me, and I was young enough to confuse recklessness with adventure.

* * *

Many of my mementos are small things I thought I had lost or misplaced, but later discovered when I least expected it: snapshots from a day of fishing I'd almost forgotten; a wad of wool for tying yarn flies on a steelhead trip lived long ago; a little bell that belonged to my sweet-natured Brittany; the key to a hunting shack I took for granted until it was gone.

Squirrel tails and gobbler beards; splintered canoe paddles and tattered fishing vests. The litany of our mementos is limited only by the number of days we spend afield, enjoying the things we most enjoy doing, in the places where we'd rather be than anywhere else in the world.

No one knows what tomorrow holds—we cross our fingers, close our eyes, and hope. But we always have yesterday with its many satisfactions, as near as the big brookie mounted on the den wall, or the bundle of deer tags hanging from a barn beam.

The day will come when I'll stop collecting pebbles and pinecones; until then I'll continue to find room on my bookshelves for tail feathers, and make new acquisitions for the collection of dried rabbit skins and mummified fish heads that adorn my garage. Perhaps by then, my wife will learn to live with the deer skull I keep on our mantle: it sits below Peg's treasured watercolor of St. Peter's Basilica—a painting she insisted we purchase from a street artist on the Ponte Sant'Angelo in Rome. We all have our mementos.

One man's treasure is another man's trash, yet the maps that guide us back through time are rarely made of ink and paper. Yesterday is never lost for those of us who keep mementos.

TWENTY-SEVEN

The Trail Not Taken

Ten years had passed since I'd last seen Phil. Back then, the two of us had worked together in the same, big-city office while sharing our daydreams about the Northwoods. Over the water cooler we'd have spirited debates about the Brule's steelhead runs, the bluebills on Bark Bay, and the big bucks of Bibon Marsh. But mostly we talked about the lark life could be if only we lived in the Lake Superior country.

In those days I was a young husband and new father who had left the North hoping to make a better life for his family. I climbed aboard the corporate caboose, bound for a steady paycheck and pension. But "better," as I was to discover, should never be measured in things you can quantify. Fortunately, I kept our cabin in the woods and in the ensuing years it was where I would go whenever I could get away—a place where I could keep in touch with the life I had traded for a company car.

Occasionally Phil accompanied me on weekend getaways to the cabin. He seldom bagged or creeled anything—usually he slept late and then spent his time talking about the life he planned to live in the woods. He would hunt and fish every day, canoe whitewater rivers, hike the North Country Trail, and sleep on balsam boughs under rock ledges just like Nessmuk.

"All I need is enough money for a grubstake," he said. "Just enough to see me through the first year. Hell, I'd even cut pulp to live in the woods."

When our company suddenly closed its regional office, the two of us were offered positions in Illinois. Phil immediately moved to suburban Chicago, but I decided to stay behind.

The move would have meant more money, but it also meant less time: less time with my family; less time for indolence and daydreams; less time to follow some untrammeled forest trail to wherever it might lead.

Instead, I took a job with a small company that allowed me to work from home—wherever home might be. Personal computers and fax machines had just arrived on the scene, and the new technology was changing everything about the workaday world. Within a month, I sold my townhouse and moved north. The cut in salary and security were substantial, but I was free to work the hours I liked and to spend at least part of each day outdoors. Meanwhile, I borrowed from Peter to keep Paul at bay, and bought my tackle from the bait shop's bargain bin.

Phil and I stayed in touch, sporadically. We'd trade cards at Christmas and exchange e-mails. I'd send the real estate brochures he always requested, and occasionally call him with an invitation if the fishing was hot. He never came. Then, last November, he had the chance to travel north on business to Duluth, Minnesota, not far from my home; afterward, he dropped by the cabin for a long weekend. We would hunt bluebills in the mornings and fish the Brule in the afternoon. But first there was catching up to do.

Phil was now head of marketing, earning the kind of salary I could only imagine. He lunched with celebrity athletes and was planning to visit Alaska as soon as he could get away—which wouldn't be any time soon, given his schedule. In fact, he hadn't cast a line or fired a gun in years. But his annual bonuses made up for that, he said.

Something nagged at me as I listened—that shrill, small voice from deep inside that cries with admonishment whenever you second-guess the choices you've made.

Stay or leave. Sink roots or soar. Be a minnow in a reservoir or a big bass in a small pond. These are the choices we face. If we're lucky, we choose wisely and never look back. But regardless of the path we pick, there forever remains the trail not taken. We never really know if the life we choose is the best we might have made.

Phil looked great, like a model in a Dunn's catalogue, sporting new wool camo and a sleek Benelli shotgun. I felt a little shabby in my frayed, brown camouflage with burlap patches on the elbows. The slide on my ancient Ithaca rattled like a sack of broken walnut shells.

I didn't say much when it was my turn to tout accomplishments.

"I fish and hunt a lot," was most of what I said.

"Someday I'm going to live like this," Phil told me. "Build a cabin. Live in the woods. Fish or hunt everyday. I'm just waiting for the right time to make the break."

* * *

The next morning he was up at 4:00 A.M., feeding oak chunks to the woodstove.

"It's *sleeting*," he said.

"The bluebills won't care."

"Yeah, but I don't shoot straight when I'm hypothermic. If you don't mind, I'll wait around here for a bit."

I left him and went down to the blind with the decoys and gun. It was too wet for good hunting and by ten o'clock the sleet had turned to a steady, gray rain. I bagged two ringbills and then went back to the cabin to check on Phil. He was sitting in front of the TV, watching a duck-hunting video.

"Ready for some fishing?" I asked.

Phil looked out at the aspens stained with rain, the bare trees snapping like whips in the wind.

"Let's do lunch," he said. "Maybe the rain will stop by the time we're finished."

I broiled the ringbill breasts while Phil concocted duck sauce from a recipe he'd found in an old Bradford Angier book. After lunch, Phil went back to his video and I visited the Brule in the rain. I didn't connect with any salmon or steelhead, but neither did Phil. He never left the cabin.

* * *

That evening, the TV news forecast rain for the next several days.

"Lousy luck," said Phil. "I should probably head home anyway. Maybe next time the weather will cooperate."

In the morning we loaded his SUV as bluebills passed overhead. Phil pointed an imaginary shotgun at the birds.

"Easy pickings," he said. Then he took a long, last look at the cabin, like a tourist who knows he won't be coming back.

I stood in the dirt road until Phil's SUV was out of sight, thinking about the different trails we'd taken, and about which of us was the luckiest. You can't wait for perfect timing or ideal weather if you want to fish and hunt—or if you want to live the life you dream about. All you can do is take a chance. The only real regret is to never risk it.

TWENTY-EIGHT

The Spook in the Timber

I'd been hunting snowshoe rabbits, forgetting about the time and ignoring the gathering dark. Now I was making the long walk home through the woods, with only the light of a full moon to guide me.

It had snowed a little just before sunset; under the brilliant moon, snowy balsams gleamed. The temperature was dropping, getting too cold to travel slowly; I tried to quicken my step, the three rabbits in my game pocket feeling as heavy as bricks. I left the alder swamps and climbed a ridge where the winds had winnowed away the deep snow. Below the ridge, a little stream had frozen in place on its way toward Lake Superior. I lingered at the top of the ravine to catch my breath.

The icy night's stunning silence was dazzling; the only sound was my laboring breath. I stared into the dark chasm of the creek, listening to the silence with all my senses, hoping to catch a glimpse of a brush wolf or bobcat. Instead, the night suddenly came to life with the call of a great horned owl.

The bird was very near and I was startled by the sound, a great booming cry that seemed to come from the night itself. I have friends who claim the ghostly call of an owl can turn their blood to slush, but for me that haunting cry speaks of something else.

An owl's call at eventide reminds me of all those winsome and wintry evenings I have known in the North—of clear, frigid nights brilliant with hoarfrost and moonlight; the bestial moaning of frozen lakes making ice under the stars; the audible shock of aspens exploding from the crepuscular cold; and lonesome ski trails deep in the woods with only the hooting of a solitary owl to keep me company. My mind is filled with the memories of such moments, and of the peace and joy I found there. But an owl's call on a winter's evening also reminds me of things I can't comprehend.

Perhaps it's because an owl's mad hooting stirs our subconscious in a way we'd just as soon ignore, reminding us of a time when we were something less than men. I once visited an archaeological dig whose former inhabitants had been cannibals: heaps of bones and human skulls lay below the rotting palisades encircling the ancient village. It reminded me of the bits of bones and tiny skulls I'd once found at the base of an old ash tree—a tree that was much favored by owls.

It's these dark images an owl's call can conjure, and the reason why owls have always been the objects of legends and myths. The Kwakiutl people of the Pacific Northwest believed that owls could call a man by name, and if the man heard the summons he would die by the next full moon. Finns in the Lake Superior country claim an owl roosting on a roof is a sure sign death will visit that house within a fortnight. And a friend of mine—a university professor from Eastern Europe—will quickly sign herself with the cross of Christ should she hear an owl. The gesture, she claims, will ward away the evil an owl's call promises to bring.

In daylight I easily smile at superstition; but on winter nights, when I'm alone on a forest trail and hear that spook cry out from deep in the dark timber, old instincts rise and flood my reason, filling me with foreboding about what may be lurking around the trail's next bend. I turn up my collar to try and shake off the chill. I tell myself it's only the press of winter I feel.

I know, of course, that the ghastly cries are simply part of an owl's courtship when the new year begins. Unlike most birds, owls mate and lay their eggs in winter, hatching their young in the blizzards of March. To the skunk and hare, an owl's cry is a harbinger of doom. But for me, an owl's call on a February evening is a promise of life to come.

An owl's call weaves its way across the frozen and inanimate landscape of winter to the tentative, first days of spring, when young owlets will fill the nest. It calls across time to the lush, green days of summer, and to nocturnal hunting forays beneath the frosty beacon of a Hunter's Moon. It calls to late November and the darkest nights of the year, and to the impression of wings straddling rabbit tracks that halt abruptly in the snow. It calls, unceasingly, as it always has to end where it begins—in the deep snows of midwinter and the start of a new year.

Now, standing at the top of the ravine above the creek, I heard another owl call from the far side of the chasm. I had the sense of seeing the great bird glide through the dark to my side of the stream. Soon two owls were calling in the unearthly way that owls do on solitary winter evenings. I held my breath, listening to the spooky maunderers, and then hurried home, knowing the cries were the sound of tomorrow—and perhaps feeling a bit relieved that tonight was not to be the night when the owl will call my name.

TWENTY-NINE

By Dawn's Early Light

Like every red-blooded American, I'm an optimist—especially at dawn on a stretch of stream or swale. It doesn't matter if my expectations are impractical. When goose season arrives ahead of the geese, I'll waddle out to the blind with two full boxes of goose loads—and at the end of the day I'll tote two, unused boxes of goose loads back to the car. Yet, come morning, I'll be as eager as ever to repeat the ritual. I know the geese won't be there, but they might be—and that's what counts.

Anything seems possible by dawn's early light, when the wraiths that addle our sleep vanish like mist before the sun. I'm as hopeful at dawn on the last day of duck season as I was at the start of opening day. And if the woodcock come spiraling down at dusk to settle in for the night among the popples behind my cabin, you'll know where to find me at daybreak.

In my corner of Wisconsin, optimism floods its banks on or about April Fool's Day, when the steelhead season opens at sunrise. This far north, the rotting snow will be knee-deep along the Brule River, and the water is apt to look and feel like a chocolate malt. The steelhead won't run upstream in great numbers until Lake Superior sheds its ice, and not one man in fifty will hook a fish on opening day. Still, anglers crowd the Brule's banks at dawn like gamblers at a dice game. There's always the chance you'll be that one man in fifty, and that makes all the difference in the world.

You never know if a man is really the optimist he seems to be until the going gets tough. Adversity can bring out the best in people.

I remember one opener on the Brule when a friend and I came to the river in a downpour. The incessant rain washed away the snow and transformed the trails into quagmires. We struggled along muddy banks through the ashen light of early dawn, the ooze sucking the boots from our heels at every step. By the time we reached the spot where I always begin to fish, we were blistered, bespattered, and bedraggled. I could hear my friend's teeth chattering as the first hint of daylight pierced the gloom.

"Do you want to go back and dry out?" I asked.

"Heck, no!" he said. "I'm wet, cold, and in pain—it doesn't get any better than this. Let's fish!"

Now *there* was an optimist.

The optimism that is there in the quiet and hopeful minutes before dawn's first light is when I daydream about the guns I hope to own someday. When it's too dark to start shooting and I'm alone with my thoughts on a marsh, I begin thinking about all the easy shots I've recently missed and how effortlessly the problem could be solved with the right gun. I already own several modest shotguns—not including the blackpowder and antique pieces I've picked up—but what I really need is a custom-fitted Orvis Waterfowler. My wife fears my optimism will land us in the poorhouse, and our son worries he'll have to quit school and get a job. They don't see how a Krieghoff or Perazzi could possibly be an investment for our future, but I do—I'm an optimist.

Optimism doesn't cost anything. It's a gift anyone can give. I've known plenty of men who worked two jobs to keep their families afloat, and still had nothing more to give their sons but a hand-me-down shotgun and a firm belief that tomorrow would be a better day.

My own father was one of them. Among the few treasures he called his own was a patch of swale a farmer let him hunt in exchange for help in making hay. Pheasants always cackled in that grass before the sun burned away the frost. We'd hit it while a few stars still gleamed in the dawn of weekend mornings so that Dad could be home by noon for his second job.

We didn't have a dog, my father's free time was scant, and the two of us shared one gun; still, he'd let me bag the day's first bird before taking his turn with the shotgun. One Saturday I made clean misses on the first two roosters we kicked up. After that I insisted Dad take the gun.

"Nope, you shoot until you bag a bird," he said. "That's the deal we have."

"But it's almost noon," I protested. "You won't get a chance to hunt."

"I am hunting," he told me. "I'm just not *shooting*. Besides, there's always tomorrow."

That swale was where I got to know my father, and where I learned about things like devotion, self-sacrifice, keeping your word when it hurts, and hope. All of which is a pretty good definition of sportsmanship—and what it means to be an American.

Yesterday was the first opener on the Brule since 9/11. Like so much else in recent life, I wasn't sure what to expect. Men huddled in the gravel parking lots waiting for daybreak, trading jokes and sharing coffee with other anglers who once would have been considered competitors on the river. Adversity had changed that.

The cheery camaraderie and sunny confidence were contagious. I liked the optimism I heard, whether it was in talking about the weather, the prospects for fishing, or the likelihood that life will someday return to the way it was before madmen came hurtling out of our skies. Then the sun began to rise in an overcast sky and we went our separate ways, down to the river and into whatever lay ahead, sure that the clouds would break.

You cannot put a great hope in a small soul, someone once said. And no endeavor will succeed without faith. Hope always burns brightest at dawn's early light—it's the stuff of sportsmen's dreams, and the steel that is America.

THIRTY

Bridges

In early May, when budding maples on distant hillsides burst into a haze of pastel colors, and stream banks were bright and yellow with cowslips, we'd load the canoes and head for the Lost Land Lakes. They're known by a different name today, but remain much the same—a group of glacial tarns and ponds linked by portage trails.

On Friday night we'd pitch camp in the dark beside Sawmill Lake, using our cars' headlights to illuminate the site while we worked. There was no exact number to our crew, though its core was made up of my dad and uncles, their sons, several cousins, and three canoes. Our excuse for these annual outings was the opening day of fishing season; but the real reasons were the Lost Land Lakes themselves and the portage trails that linked them.

We slept in big, canvas tents that reeked with that distinctive odor only canvas tents possess, with nothing but the flickering light of a campfire to keep the shadows at bay. The men in our group fell asleep as soon as they curled up in their sleeping bags, but none of us kids could sleep. All through the night, we'd lie awake listening to the trembling wailing of loons and the incessant din of spring peepers, the little frogs sounding for all the world like distant sleigh bells. The older kids among us delighted in torturing little cousins with tales of ghosts and terror each time a branch snapped in the haunted forest behind us. When the youngest kids began to cry, one of our uncles in the other tent would stir to shout at us—"Go to sleep or I'll come in there and you'll really have something to cry about!"

At daylight we'd make breakfast, load the canoes, and shove off before the morning mists burned away. We'd make the long carry over Ghost Portage into Beartrap Lake, where one of my uncles had a favorite bay he fished for pike; then the rest of us would continue to our own fond places, paddling across blue lakes that reflected the sunrise. We weaved our way through the greasy muck of portage trails, where last year's dried aspen leaves crackled like wrapping paper beneath our sneakers. In a way, those portage trails were like a gift wrapped in paper, our every step peeling away the packaging to reveal yet another surprise.

We let the adults do the serious fishing—my brothers and cousins had no patience with sitting in a motionless canoe while staring at lifeless cork bobbers. Instead, we'd walk the portage trails or paddle a fiberglass tub from one wilderness lake to the next, pressing ever deeper into the woods, lured by the calling of loons and the thrill of unfettered freedom. There, on the Lost Land Lakes, with miles of unvisited woods and water all around us, a boy in a canoe was as free as the clouds in the sky.

* * *

By mid-morning, the men in our clan would walk the trails searching for us. We couldn't wander through that lake-speckled country without crossing each other's paths: a dad helping a pair of youngsters make the long carry into Telstar Lake; two uncles challenging their nephews to a canoe race across Long Pond; a teenager stopping to pull his little cousin out of the quagmire of

Muskeg Portage. These meanderings among the Lost Land Lakes taught us more about each other than it ever did about the out-of-doors.

It was on the lakes and portage trails where the decorum of daily life vanished. Uncles would lie in ambush, pelting nephews with pinecones when their canoe passed too close to shore. Cousins would tie together the bootlaces of a dozing uncle, and then splash him awake with a hat full of water. In the ensuing melee, one of us kids would be dragged down to the shore to be dunked by his heels in an icy lake. Then the loons would begin to move, calling wildly from out of the blue above us, calling us back across the portages and ponds.

The opening day of fishing season brought us together in a way that nothing else could. Back home, we met at weddings, baptisms, and birthday parties, but the settings were different and, because of that, we were different, too. But in the woods and on the portage trails of opening day, we were more than just a group of people who shared the same history or name. We were more than just friends and relatives—we were family.

* * *

People don't stay put anymore—I'm as guilty of that as anyone; and although our family stays in touch, it is no longer as large, or extended, or clannish. These days, Dad does his fishing from a dock; my uncles have retired to distant desert cities. Long ago my cousins fled south like teal in August, and my brothers haven't made an opening day in years—there doesn't seem to be as much time anymore. Only my sister's son shows up on opening day.

Now, making the long carry across Ghost Portage with my young nephew, I know he would like the canvas tents and spooky stories, the canoe races and pinecone fights, and the pranks his uncles played on their elders. I wish, as we set our canoe into Beartrap Lake, that he may yet discover what I found in this Lost Land. The portages I traipsed as a child were more than just links between lakes; they were the bridges that made us a family, leading us to the place where we belonged, and where I still linger on opening day.

THIRTY-ONE

Home from the Hill

These days I seldom get to bed early, unless I'll be hunting or fishing the next day. Even then, I'll be the one who banks the fire and turns out the lights long after everyone else is asleep. It's late at night, alone in the deepening dark and calm, that I tend to think back to times and places I've known in the out-of-doors—those treasured small pleasures I recall with affection, and to which I return when I can't sleep.

These memories are the riches I've accumulated—the little somethings I've saved and set aside for rainy days and my old age. Every now and then—like tonight—I like to go over my portfolio. Financial planners suggest a conservative investor allocate his assets evenly between common stocks and bonds. I try to follow their advice by maintaining a 50/50 mix of hunting and fishing memories.

In financial terms, I'm somewhere between broke and treading water. But in terms of things I can understand, I'm as comfortable as a king. Who else but a king can return at will to a cedar-rimmed pool on the Flag River where the trout grow as long as your leg? And I doubt if even Camelot had the kind of boggy meadow where I once bagged a limit of snipe in two hours.

I have no illusions: By anyone's standards, my fortune is picayune. But if happy memories were fairly valued, I'd be listed on the DJIA. But since the chances of that happening are slim, I'll continue to follow forest trails instead of financial trends. I'm a great believer in the ancient admonishment to store up riches where neither rust nor moth nor thief can enter: "For where your treasure is, there too will your heart be."

* * *

The lifetime annuity I acquired this year was seeing my son take his first deer. It happened in the last five minutes of the season. Nick was thinking about climbing down from his stand and calling it quits, when he spotted the animal moving soundlessly through the dusky popples on the far side of a swamp, 100 yards away. It was almost dark, he was hunting over iron sights with a .30-30, and the only clear shot through the trees was at the animal's neck. He squeezed the trigger, expecting the buck to bound away; instead, the deer dropped to the ground. For once I was in the right place at the right time: the look of joy and satisfaction I saw on Nick's face happens only once in the life of a boy. But the memory of that deer will be paying dividends to the two of us for years to come.

This year's catch-up contribution to my 401(k) was a trip I'd been putting off for years. Finally, last May, I convinced Peg that a trip to the Arctic watershed was really an investment, and how its total return—calculated on a pro forma basis—would easily justify my purchase of a new reel and rod. On a branch of the Flint River, I caught 2-pound brookies as easily as if they were fish in a fountain; and on a lake near the Chipman I caught and released more walleyes than I could count. We did suffer a long-term loss, however, when the tip of my new rod snapped off. Just as I can't remember to buy low and sell high, I forget to walk around windfalls instead of barging through them.

Total yield on my nontraditional IRA this year was a dozen bluebills I took from potholes north of the Totagatic River. Twice I came across potholes teeming with scaup, their numbers so vast that from a distance the lakes looked black and studded with stumps. When the bluebills realized I was there they rose as one, the teeming flocks rising up into the sky and—for a few breathless moments—actually blotting out the sun. I don't know if this sort of thing is still common in other places, but I've come to expect it living in the Lake Superior country.

Here, where the hunting and fishing is still as good as it used to be, you can wander for days in any direction and know you'll have all those many miles to yourself. There are pockets of it where trout streams outnumber roads, and in much of it deer are more plentiful than people. Here, where solitude is never far away, the wild is always calling. That's why, years ago, Peg and I chose to make our home and start our family within casting distance of Lake Superior. In terms of total return, it's been the best investment we ever made.

* * *

This year's Christmas bonus was a 30-inch steelhead I caught during the first storm of winter. It was exhilarating to be alone in a stark and frozen wilderness, fishing a gray stream framed in white snow and black spruce. I felt like a character from a Jack London story, trying to prove to the elements that I could be chastened but never crushed. The steelhead glistened like a gem against the pure snow, silver and bright with a vivid pink stripe the length of its flanks. I was tempted to keep it. But in the end, I released the steelhead to earn a bit more interest on my investment. I wrote it off as a year-end contribution to my favorite charity: Many More Fish for Tomorrow.

A few items in my portfolio have turned out to be laggards instead of the sure bets I thought they would be: the new woodcock cover I found has thus far produced more rabbits than birds; the lightweight canoe I purchased has become just as heavy to carry as the fiberglass bathtub it replaced; and the case of Fasteel in which I invested shoots as far behind a speeding teal as did the steel shot I used last season. Friends insist it's not the shot but the shooter who's slowing down.

One of those friends is an attorney. Whenever the walleyes take a break from biting, he reminds me I need a will to preserve and pass on my estate; but I doubt my memories will end up in probate. Still, I've been giving some consideration to what people used to call "last things"—those things few of us plan for but none of us escape.

An old bear guide I used to hunt with once said that instead of a tombstone he wanted someone to plant a tree on his grave. It's an idea that appeals to me. I'm partial to shaggy white cedars and hemlocks. But before I set that down in my last will and testament, I need to decide upon a final resting place.

"You're being morbid," Peg told me when I mentioned the subject.

"I'm planning for the future," I said. "Like our plans to see Alaska when we retire."

"People come back from Alaska," Peg said.

"I'll write your eulogy," offered our son. A future English professor, he strikes me as being a bit too eager to pen an elegy to me.

* * *

Still, I've been thinking of what I would like in the way of an epitaph. It doesn't need to be profound, clever, or humorous; it doesn't even have to be original. All I want are a few words to explain why I spent so much time staring up into the slate-colored skies above my mallard decoys, when I should have been peering over financial statements and balance sheets. I want to make it clear I wasn't wasting time in visiting all those many deer stands and bass lakes, while most of my peers were visiting their C.P.A.

Until tonight it seemed hopeless. But after everyone was asleep, and the house grew as quiet as the hush that is there just before dawn, I sat down with a pipe, a bit of Black Bush, and a book of poems, and realized that what I wanted to say had been said years ago by Robert Louis Stevenson. I don't know if Stevenson was a sportsman, but his poem, "Requiem," could be an epitaph for every man who lives and loves the outdoor life:

> Under the wide and starry sky
> Dig the grave and let me lie:
> Glad did I live and gladly die,
> And I laid me down with a will.
>
> This be the verse you grave for me:
> *Here he lies where he long'd to be;*
> *Home is the sailor, home from the sea,*
> *And the hunter home from the hill.*

THIRTY-TWO

The Secret of Chequah-Bikwaki

Winter was all but gone from the woods when I visited Thunder Mountain. The snow lay only in patches, at the bottom of deep hollows and on the sheltered north sides of hills. In the wake of the thaw tiny streams roared like torrents, while little lakes were blue pools of restless water under windswept skies. Only the largest lakes remained solid, trapped and held captive by the lingering ice.

To a geologist, Thunder Mountain is only a monadnock, an isolated ridge of bedrock that towers above the glacial-scarred country between the north and south forks of Wisconsin's Thunder River, but to the Old Ones who first knew and loved the North—the Chippewa, Potawatomi, and Menomonee—Thunder Mountain was a holy place of legends and superstition. To them it was *Chequah-Bikwaki*, home of the great Thunderbirds, the guardian spirits of men.

Although its wilderness character had changed since the days of the Thunderbirds, the mountain was still wild and primitive. It was a favorite place of sportsmen and weekend vacationers, but now, in early spring, it stood alone. In a few days I would be meeting friends at the confluence of the nearby Thunder and Peshtigo rivers; but until then, I wanted to spend some time alone with the mountain and perhaps capture a little of its ancient mysteries and myths.

The Old Ones knew there was more to a land than geology. To them, Thunder Mountain was a place of spirits, wielding the power to change men's souls. They told of such things in ways not easily understood, guarding the secrets of the spirit world against those who saw only a mountain. Sometimes the meanings of the myths are unclear, but the feelings such stories stir remain changeless. Like the cry of loons or the howling of wolves, an Indian legend speaks to the heart.

They told of windigos, giant monsters made of ice who prowled the winter woods below the mountain hunting human flesh. To destroy a windigo, it was necessary for a man to become a windigo himself and try to kill the creature by shattering its icy shell. There was seldom joy when the monster was defeated, however: At the core of every windigo was the lifeless body of an ordinary man, a captive of the icy cast. Any man could become a windigo if his heart turned cold and black.

Other tales tell of a time when there was no such thing as death. In those days, the world and everything in it lived in harmony, except for the rivalry between two serpents. One day the two serpents slipped into a garden where a young couple was sitting. In a test to see which snake was more powerful, the horned serpent tricked his rival into striking one of them. When nothing happened, the horned snake struck the other, and that youth died instantly. Because the snake had brought death into the world, he was shunned by men and condemned to live in the low places beneath the mountain forever. There he dwells as a symbol of all that is evil, the archenemy of the glorious Thunderbirds. Though details vary from one place to the next, the tale is a story that everyone knows.

* * *

I was thinking of the old legends as I climbed Thunder Mountain, wondering what I expected to find at the top. It was only a hill, much like any other, and yet I felt drawn to it as an explorer following a stream to its source. I had no expectations about what I might discover; at best, I hoped to find some clue as to why men once believed that Thunderbirds had nested on the crest. Even if I failed to find that, there was still the pleasure of being abroad in the final days of winter, alone with an old and wild mountain in the moment before the wilderness erupted into spring.

Halfway to the top, I stopped to rest and look out at the world below. Color was slowly coming back into the stark, wintry country. Distant poplars were brushed with an apple-green haze, the color so light and soft it seemed suspended in the trees, like clouds of woodsmoke. I remembered the five-mile walk I once made through those same woods, flushing more than a dozen partridges—and missing every shot—until I doubled on woodcock. Another time, on a high ridge where budding maples were pink as a winter sunset, I once walked a large whitetail into the ground before jumping the buck in his bed. My mind was filled with memories of the Thunder Mountain country, experiences that, in one way or another, had shaped my thoughts and perceptions as a man. Although I might never know the secret of *Chequah-Bikwaki*, the mountain had long ago worked its magic on my life.

Then I heard the robin calling. It was the first of the season, singing in a balsam copse above me, the music fluid as water gurgling in a brook. I listened to the singing while basking in the warm sunlight, filled with peace and quiet anticipation. The robin signaled the approach of a time when the woods would again be lush and green, when hot air would buzz with the whine of insects and trout lurk in ambush beneath the deceptive calm of forest pools.

In the tales of the old Chippewa, the robin heralds a metamorphosis, a transition from death to life. Now, sitting in the early spring sunshine on Thunder Mountain, it was easy for me to grasp the meaning of that myth: Winter was over, and things were changing as the earth began to beat with new life.

To the Old Ones, the wilderness that was *Chequah-Bikwak* was a place of power, for the mountain was not only a barrier but also a bridge: a bridge between rivers, between hunting grounds, between people, and, most of all, between the realm of spirit and the everyday world of men. The Old Ones who ventured near the mountain in quest of its secret did so in silence, out of reverence for the Thunderbirds nesting at its crest. When they returned to their villages, they said little of their discoveries, though everyone knew that the mountain had worked its magic on those men.

* * *

It was almost dark when I reached the crest, and in the twilight the mountain seemed to belong to another world. Like all places of legends and superstition, the crest had a sense of mystery, and I could understand why men once believed that Thunderbirds dwelled among the dark timber of the mountaintop. Sitting alone among its trees and rocks, I wondered what strange and forgotten things had happened there to hallow that ground. I listened for the Thunderbirds, longing to learn the secret; there was only the eternal silence of the rocks.

Suddenly, from far away, I heard the baying of Canada geese. I searched the sky as their calling grew sharp and shrill; then I saw the wedge of the flock, frail as a cobweb, etched in black against the rising moon. In a moment they vanished, but for long afterward their din was an eerie chant as the mountain throbbed with their calls. The Canadas were moving north again, bringing spring in their tow and enchantment to the night.

The calling of the geese enthralled me. Long after the birds disappeared, I stood on the mountain's crest, marveling at the mystery of wild things and places, thinking that maybe, if I listened long enough, I might find a clue to the magic of that place. I found no answers to the riddle of migration, no hint of the unseen force that compelled the geese to move north with the receding snows. Instead, there was a feeling of having been a part of their mysterious passage. That—and perhaps something of the same awe the Old Ones experienced when they ventured to *Chequah-Bikwaki*.

Like an Indian legend, the calling of the geese touched something deep in my heart, and when it did, I felt as close to the Thunderbirds as a modern man could. In that moment, I understood the secret of *Chequah-Bikwaki* and why the Old Ones guarded it by creating superstitions and myths.

The secret is that wilderness has the power to breathe life into the human spirit, a spirit meant to dwell in high places even Thunderbirds could not ascend. That is the magic and meaning of wild places. Man may not preserve the wilderness, but surely wilderness preserves man.

About the Author

Jack Kulpa lives in Wisconsin, near the wilderness lakes and forests of the Lake Superior country. He has been a regular contributor to *Field & Stream* for more than twenty years, and has written hundreds of articles for America's top outdoor magazines. An award-winning writer, his stories on fishing and hunting, outdoor life, and the need to preserve wild places are included in anthologies. *Gray's Sporting Journal* has called him "one of the great voices of the North Woods," and *Sports Afield* ranks his work among "the greatest outdoor writing of the twentieth century." His book, *True North: Reflections on Fishing and a Life Well Lived,* received the Ellis-Henderson Outdoor Writing Award.